OUR AMERICAN CARDINALS

OUR AMERICAN CARDINALS

LIFE STORIES OF THE SEVEN AMERICAN CARDINALS
MC CLOSKEY, GIBBONS, FARLEY, O'CONNELL, DOUGHERTY, MUNDELEIN, HAYES

BY

JAMES J. WALSH
M.D., PH.D., LITT.D., K.C.ST.G.

MEDICAL DIRECTOR OF FORDHAM UNIVERSITY SCHOOL OF SOCIAL SERVICE;
PROFESSOR OF PHYSIOLOGICAL PSYCHOLOGY, CATHEDRAL COLLEGE,
NEW YORK; AUTHOR OF "THE THIRTEENTH—GREATEST OF
CENTURIES," "THE WORLD'S DEBT TO THE CATHOLIC
CHURCH," "PSYCHOTHERAPY," "CURES," ETC.

*The ideal is not a dream but your practical
duty of every day.*

CARDINAL MERCIER.

D. APPLETON AND COMPANY
NEW YORK :; 1926 :: LONDON

1337

PRINTED IN THE UNITED STATES OF AMERICA

TO THE MEMORY OF
OUR FIRST AMERICAN CARDINAL
JOHN, CARDINAL McCLOSKEY
OF NEW YORK

INTRODUCTION

Cardinals are the highest ecclesiastics in the Roman Catholic Church next to the Pope. The word cardinal comes from the Latin word *cardo,* a hinge, which is probably derived from the Greek κραδᾶν swing, and the cardinals are the hinges on which swing the authority of the Church throughout the world. They are chosen from the various countries more or less according to the number of Catholics among the various peoples and the dignity of the episcopal sees which they hold. They are members of what is known as the Sacred College of Cardinals and act as counselors to the Pope in the government of the Church. On the death of the Pope the ecclesiastical authority devolves on them and they administer the Church's faculties, shape its policies and protect the Church's interests until the election of a new Pope. They are appointed by the Pope and are of three classes or orders, cardinal bishops, six in number, cardinal priests, fifty in number, and cardinal deacons, fourteen in all. Vacancies nearly always exist in the College of Cardinals and the full number of seventy is seldom complete.

Cardinals the world over undoubtedly represent more fully than any other members of the hierarchy the spirit of the Church. Hence sketches of the lives of cardinals that we have had here in the United States down to the present time comprise the most trustworthy and absolutely reliable evidence as to the attitude of the Church toward this country and toward American ideals. They were chosen for advancement to the second highest dignity in the Church after years of service which served to reveal their characters and proclaim what their influence was likely to be. Almost needless to say under these circumstances while they were always outstanding factors in the religious life of their day they were not always the most brilliantly intellectual but were chosen for the qualities of their hearts and souls as well as of their heads. Mr. Bertrand Russell reminded us not long since that we still have need for that word "heart" in psychology, for by it we mean those qualities of mankind through which men express "the sum total of kindly impulses" and thoughtfulness for others. He added, that where these kindly impulses exist and are developed "science helps them to be effective; where they are absent science only makes men more cleverly diabolic."

While all of our American cardinals have been

broadly cultured men in the best sense of that word and most of them have impressed themselves deeply on their generation by their intellectual qualities, none of them had the advantage of what is so often considered to be necessary for culture, early home influences in the midst of family life where ease and plenty provided opportunities for special æsthetic development. All of our American cardinals have come from among the people and have known a little something at least of straitened circumstances in their early years. Most of them had that very precious experience which Thucydides, the great Greek historian, valued so highly, of having to go through hard things when they were young. If it were only the ecclesiastical seminaries of the older days, with their stern strict discipline, and their, to say the least, utter simplicity of food and accommodations, the American cardinals when young were subjected to conditions which that wise old Greek with his knowledge of men thought more likely to develop character and personality than any others. For Thucydides declared that the majority of men are possessed of about the same human qualities and only a few of them rise above the average of mankind because they had to submit to hardships in their youth.

Our American cardinals have not been men who

have been in the public eye except in so far as their ecclesiastical duties at various times during life happen to evoke publicity. As a rule they have been least of all publicity seekers in any sense of that term. They have been simple, sincere men known for their fidelity to the practice of religious duties, and for their readiness to make sacrifices in the cause that they had most at heart. Sacrifice is the primary essence of religion. Above all, these men have been noteworthy for their readiness to be helpful to others just as far as in them lay. The one quality that has stood out in the lives of all the American cardinals has been profound thoughtfulness for others and a notable lack of anything like selfishness.

A great saint once said, "Show me some one who forgets himself or herself completely and I will show you some one whom the world will not willingly forget." The men destined to be cardinals here in the United States have done the next thing that came to hand in the course of duty just as well as possible and after a while they have wakened up to the fact that the world was paying attention to them and that their ecclesiastical superiors recognized the worth of their personalities. Brought up in a republic where every man necessarily learns some lessons in politics, there has been almost none of the politician in them. One ecclesiastical position after another was fulfilled so well that advancement has naturally come to the next. They have been told, "Friend, come up higher." Not infrequently they have taken a place that was being striven for by others though they had not realized at times the pressure around them.

In a well-known passage Robert Louis Stevenson, contrasting the position that the physician and the clergyman hold in relation to their fellow mortals, expressed a view that is perhaps rather common among those situated like Stevenson himself, who know clergymen very little and, from force of circumstances because they are ill, know much about physicians. He said, "There are men and classes of men that stand above the common herd: the soldier, the sailor, and the shepherd not infrequently; the artist rarely; rarelier still, the clergymen; the physician almost as a rule." This very flattering contrast for the physician is not often expressed by Stevenson's colleagues among literary men, but on the contrary they are prone to deprecate the physician and from Molière and even earlier down to our own day have been very ready to impugn his motives and contemn his science. It is a question of intimate knowledge. From Stevenson later in the South Seas after he had come to know Father Damien, the leper priest of Molokai, we had highest words of praise for a clergyman. I have the feeling that all that is needed to have Catholic clergymen thoroughly appreciated is to know them well. "The man I don't like is the man I don't know," is a very old expression in English that can be traced back to the Greek. Having known these American cardinals myself I am very much inclined to think that the only thing necessary for others to appreciate them properly is to know them well; hence this volume.

I feel assured that Stevenson would have found these men, had he known them well, to be among the "shepherds" who to his mind so frequently stand above the common herd   They have all been men who are intent on caring for others and especially those who most needed care   Our own cardinal in New York declared when they tendered him his first public banquet in honor of his new dignity that he would much prefer that they should think of him as the shepherd of his flock rather than the cardinal prince of the Church. Such I know from personal acquaintance are the feelings of the other cardinals of our day, as they were of our dead cardinals. They spent themselves in charity, that is not in that mere helping of the unfortunate which has sometimes in modern times been considered to be the whole meaning of the word charity, but in the cultivation of that dearness to them of other people because of the brotherhood of man and the fatherhood of God that represents the highest development of human character that we can have. Our cardinals have been men who have tried to the fullest of their power to make life for their fellowmen as happy and as whole-heartedly satisfying as it would be.

In doing so they have above all reached out their hands to those who were lowest in the social scale, they have remembered whether consciously or not Christ's expression that the greatest mark of His Church is that "the Gospel is preached to the poor." Though they belonged to what is by far the oldest aristocracy in the world, an aristocracy of character and not of birth, which has far outlived the monarchs and the dynasties, the noble families and the political institutions of all kinds throughout the civilized world, they have themselves been thoroughly democratic in their ways and in their attitude of mind toward those around them.

Our American cardinals, all of them, illustrate very well President Wilson's expression with regard to the Church as representing through her great ecclesiastics the most important element in the development and maintenance of the spirit of democracy during the Middle Ages. While he was president of Princeton and before the burden of responsibility as President of the United States came to make such well-weighed expressions on historical subjects no longer possible, Mr. Wilson paid a tribute to the Church that deserves to be recalled. Almost needless to say, after his long studies of the history of the American people and their democracy with its vicissitudes for well above a hundred years as the background of his own historical mindedness, President Wilson was eminently well fitted to have an opinion in the matter and had the right to have that opinion carry weight. He said, in the volume known as *The New Freedom,* "The only reason why government did not suffer dry rot in the Middle Ages under the aristocratic systems which then prevailed was that the men who were efficient instruments of government were drawn from the Church—from that great Church, that body which we now distinguish from other Church bodies as the Roman Catholic Church. The Roman Catholic Church then and now was a great democracy. There was no peasant so humble that he might not become a priest, and no priest so obscure that he might not become Pope of Christendom, and every chancellery of Europe was ruled by those learned, trained and accomplished men—the priest-

hood of that great and then dominant Church; and
so what kept government alive in the Middle Ages
was this constant rise of the sap from the bottom,
from the rank and file of the great body of the
people, through the open channels of the Roman
Catholic priesthood."

That very acute politician who knew men so well,
Mark Hanna, is said once to have declared that
there were two great safeguards against anarchy in
the United States, "the United States Supreme
Court and the Roman Catholic Church." In this
country there is no such union of Church and State
as would enable great Roman Catholic ecclesiastics
to be of direct political significance as they were in
the days when they ruled as the chancellors of
Europe. It was not at all with any idea as to their
political import but their moral significance that
Senator Hanna made his declaration. Even a little
study of the lives of our American cardinals makes
it very clear that they represent an abiding influence
for good among the people such as was exerted by
their colleagues of the older time to whom political
office came unsought as a rule.

The cardinal of Belgium whom Hilaire Belloc
proclaimed "the greatest figure in contemporary history" has just passed from us. His career exemplified what a great churchman can mean for his people

"I consider it a grace of God not to have had in my youth abundance, for there I learned to appreciate suffering and to understand it."

CARDINAL MERCIER

PREFACE

During recent years a great many people, noting the growth of the Roman Catholic Church in this country, have come to ask themselves and others the question, what is the place of the Catholic Church in a great liberty-loving country like ours? I think that the best answer to that question is afforded by the lives of the men who have risen to be cardinals of the Church in this country. Belgium learned in time of trial how precious a cardinal might be. May we here in the United States be spared any such rude lesson, but if so, we will not know that our cardinals are of the same stature as their leaders we shall know them.

By a fortunate coincidence I happen to have known personally all seven of the American cardinals. This has tempted me to think that perhaps I could present their lives in such a way as to make America understand their lives.

PREFACE

During recent years a great many people, noting the growth of the Roman Catholic Church in this country, have come to ask themselves and others the question, what is the place of the Catholic Church in a great liberty loving country like ours? I think that the best answer to that question is afforded by the lives of the men who have risen to be cardinals of the Church in this country. Belgium learned in time of trial how precious a cardinal might be. May we here in the United States be spared any such rude lesson, but it is well to know that our cardinals are of the same strain. By their leaders, ye shall know them.

By a fortunate coincidence I happen to have known personally all seven of the American cardinals. This has tempted me to think that perhaps I could present their lives in such a way as to make Americans understand them better.

CONTENTS

CONTENTS

ILLUSTRATIONS

OUR AMERICAN CARDINALS

JOHN, CARDINAL McCLOSKEY

First American Cardinal

THE first American cardinal, John McCloskey, archbishop of New York, was one of those gentle, charming men whom those who knew him well learned first to admire and then to love and reverence. He was in many ways a reminder of that wonderful character, St. Francis de Sales, whom so many people even when without sympathy for his apostolic labors as a great Catholic bishop, have learned to think of so reverently. Bulwer Lytton, writing to his friend, Lady Sherborne, toward the end of his life said, "I read last night the life of St. Francis de Sales. That Roman Catholic Faith, between you and me, does produce very fine specimens of adorned humanity—at once so sweet and so heroic." These are words that apply very well to our first American cardinal during his long career as a churchman here in America. He was, so far as his mind and heart were concerned, a marvelously fine specimen of "adorned humanity." His very lovable character proved gentle and patient under some of the severest trials that come to men. The heroic elements in his life were much more in evidence than might possibly be expected in the career of a man whom manifestly his superiors picked out early in life for higher things and then proceeded to afford the opportunities for such development of mind and heart as would make him adequate for them.

The future cardinal was born March 20, 1810, in what was the little town of Brooklyn, N. Y., then very different from the great "city of churches" that was to spring into existence in the years to come even before its amalgamation with the greater city of New York. I have often called attention to the fact that most of the men who do things worth while are born in small towns. Such men as Marshal Foch and Cardinal Mercier as well as Pasteur and Mendel, and ever so many other men in our time are striking examples of this, which seems to have been almost the rule of humanity down the centuries. Shakespeare was born in a little town and so were practically all the men who achieved fame in the London of his day, in Elizabethan and Jacobean times. Practically every one of the men

CARDINAL MCCLOSKEY

whom we know as Romans were born not in Rome itself but outside of it, and all the men of the Silver Age who distinguished themselves in Rome were born over in Spain. Even Athens did not give birth to its great men, but such supreme Athenians as Æschylus and Sophocles and Euripides were born outside of Athens. It is possible that the large city acts as something of an incubus on those who are brought up in it and does not permit that full development of talent as well as genius which comes so much more characteristically in the midst of the small towns where less is thought about what people will think and say as regards new developments that may occur.

His parents, Patrick McCloskey and Elizabeth Hassin, natives of Dungiven, County Derry, in the north of Ireland, came to America in 1808 after their marriage. They belonged to that rather large group of Irish people who came out to America in the generation before the famine and who made it a noteworthy distinction for themselves—as my grandmother never failed to do if occasion offered —that they had left Ireland not under the dire compulsion of necessity and starvation hanging over them but of their own free choice because they were sure that they could better themselves in this great free country and had the means to make the at-

tempt. The McCloskeys were not well-to-do, were
on the contrary in very moderate circumstances, but
they were thrifty with the spirit of the north of
Ireland and they succeeded in getting on quite well.
With the Irish worship of education they wanted
their son to have the advantage of the best possible
development of mind that they could afford. When
he was about ten their boy was sent to the leading
classical school in New York City at that time, kept
by Thomas Brady, father of James T. and John R.
Brady, who were to be so well-known in the after
life of New York. This Brady School was one of
the landmarks in education in New York in those
early days before the development of our public-
school system.

At the age of twelve John McCloskey was sent
to Mt. St. Mary's College, Emmitsburg, Md. Of
course he did not enter the college department but
the first year of the seven-year course of three
grammar classes and four college classes which then
constituted the college education of the time. A
little more than fifty years later when I entered St.
John's College, Fordham, that was still the school
and college curriculum under the French influences
which were still paramount, for St. John's was as
yet in the New York and Canada Province of the
Society of Jesus. Similar French factors were at

work at Emmitsburg where young McCloskey came
under the influence of two distinguished French
priests, both of them afterward bishops, Dubois,
who became Bishop of New York, and Bruté who
went to Bardstown, Ky. They had much to do not
only with the development of his intelligence but also
with the formation of his character. Probably nowhere in the country at that time could a boy secure
a more solid education with due training of both
intellect and will than in the "Old Mountain" as it
was affectionately called by its graduates. From it
came a great many of the Catholic bishops of the
country and probably nothing shows the worth of
Mt. St. Mary's education so well as the fact that
these bishops deeply influenced their generations
throughout the United States and built up the
American Church in accordance with the strictest
Catholicity and the highest American ideals under
conditions that were always difficult and sometimes
must have seemed almost impossible.

One of the great difficulties of the college was
transportation. This constituted also one of the
sources of efficient training of muscles and will.
The students came by stagecoach from Baltimore,
Frederick and Hanover, not minding if they had to
walk some considerable distances on the way so long
as they could ship their baggage. Long walks were

the order of that day. Father (afterward Bishop) Bruté, as president of Mt. St. Mary's, used to go in from the college to Baltimore on business at regular intervals, but did it on foot. The distance by the rude roads of the period, often little better than bridle paths, was about fifty miles. Horses were needed very much for farm work, and so the president did not feel that it was quite proper for him to take one of them away from the farm for several days. He used to start very early in the morning, dine in the middle of the day with some friends who lived some thirty miles on the way and rest for a couple of hours, and then be in Baltimore in the evening. He has been known to spend all the next day doing business errands of various kinds in Baltimore and then start back the third day for Emmitsburg, which he would reach in the evening, having walked a hundred miles and spent most of the intervening day on his feet in Baltimore. With an example like this the students must have felt that the inconveniences of travel ought to be borne as a matter of course.

Emmitsburg in those old days was undoubtedly rude in its provisions of even what might have seemed almost the necessaries of life. Here is an account of the day at "The Mountain," written by one of the Elder family with regard to life in the

college within five years of the time when young
McCloskey entered the school. Though improvements came rapidly it is doubtful whether there was
much change in the daily program before the young
Brooklyn student's introduction to boarding-school
life as it was lived in the twenties of the nineteenth
century. "We were awakened at a very early hour
in the morning (5 A.M.) by one of the prefects
walking up and down the dormitory, smacking his
hands together with a noise that could be heard all
over the house—and if any fellow was observed
playing "possum," his cot was tilted to one side and
he was unceremoniously dumped out on the floor.
As each boy finished his toilet, which was done generally in about two minutes, he went down to take
his morning ablutions at the pump, so-called, but it
was no pump at all—being simply a long trough dug
out of a solid log, pierced at both sides with a dozen
or more holes through which the water flowed con-
tinually day and night, summer and winter, and we
had only to catch two or three double handfuls of
water—souse our faces and wipe them off with a
towel with which every fellow provided himself as
he went from the dormitory. In the winter time
the feat of washing was often accompanied with
accidents that afforded fun for the fellows but no
fun for the actor. The splashing of the water,

freezing in front of the trough, formed a mound of ice just where we had to get in order to catch the water—and it was an everyday occurrence for some of us to get a fall and often to slip into the pool which was formed by the frozen spray—and many a time we found our faces fringed round with icicles formed on our hair during the short time it took us to make our ablutions on those bitter winter mornings. *

"In the winter time after washing, we had morning prayers in the big play room, but in the summer we went up to the church on the mountain to hear Mass. Then we had a short study and after that,

---

* There is a story told of one of the English public schools, the underlying experience in which could very probably have been paralleled in the Emmitsburg of those days. In the winter time there was very inadequate provision of heat, and one morning one of the small new boys, rather fresh as yet from his mother's delicate care of him, was discovered blowing on his fingers, they were so cold, and with tears running down his cheeks. The head master came along and discovered him and asked what was the matter. When the boy said that it was so cold he could not stand it, the head master said gruffly: "Well, this is no young ladies' seminary." Curiously enough, some twenty years later, when that boy, as a captain in the English army, was given the order to charge in battle under circumstances where it seemed almost inevitable that he would never come back alive, for he and his men were quite literally being sent in as a forlorn hope to save the rest of the army, he remarked to his colonel, who came from the same school, as he touched his cap after receiving the order to advance, and was just ready to lead his men, "Well, this is what old ——— [naming the head master] would say is no young ladies' seminary." The men who have to go through hard things when they are young, come out of them ready for still harder things as they grow older.

breakfast, which was a frugal repast indeed; a big bowl of good hot coffee and a hunk of bread which the boys generally broke up in the coffee—no butter —no meat nor relish of any kind. For dinner we had meat and gravy in abundance—but there was no attention paid to carving, and the whole service was of the most primitive character—but the feature of our dinners in the summer and fall, was the gumbo soup—that was luxurious—and although I have been a lover of gumbo soup ever since I learned to eat it there, it seems to me I have never found any so good as what we had at School. Supper was the same as breakfast, with the additional accompaniment occasionally of a little butter."

John McCloskey was always rather delicate in health and continued all during life to be of slight frame that would apparently not be able to stand much. The climate of Maryland was probably much more healthy for him than would have been that of any place farther north, though "The Mountain" must have been trying enough during the colder weather. His delicate constitution kept him from being interested much in college sports. They were really sports in those days and not training for games with outside colleges. There was much more time for occupation with the things of the mind because there was not so much interest in the things of the body. He was one of the best students at Mt. St. Mary's in his time, a leader in his classes, and deeply devoted to his work.

After seven years of college work, which consisted mainly of the classics and of mathematics and French as a modern language, he did his philosophy and theology during the next five years and was ordained at the age of twenty-four. He had already given abundant evidence of breadth of intellectual interest and of a mind desirous of culture and his life was to develop these very fully. For more than a generation the tradition of his gentle scholarliness continued to be one of the precious heritages of "The Mountain."

All his life John McCloskey remained one of these frail mortals who have to be careful about themselves all the time or they are likely to suffer severely from indiscretions and yet who so often succeed in accomplishing an immense deal of work and live on to a long life far beyond the average of humanity. As long ago as Plato's time it was hinted that the invalid was the long liver among men and Oliver Wendell Holmes in our time gave us the formula that for a long life probably the best thing is for a man to have some mild chronic ill which demands that he take good care of himself, for this often enables him to live on when the rashness of

the vigorous because of their exuberant health or
the indiscretions of thoughtlessness in the very
healthy often lead to premature termination of existence. Few men accomplished more in their lives
than Cardinal McCloskey though all his life he
probably felt that there were not many years ahead
of him of which he could be absolutely assured.
This uncertainty of life did not give him pause in
his work nor set him to waste of time over idle
dreads, nor the putting off of necessary developments in his diocese that were demanded by the
rapid growth of the population. He left the future
to Providence but did his work to the best possible
effect in the present.

He was ordained in old St. Patrick's Cathedral, in
New York, down on Mott Street, January 12, 1834,
the first native of New York State to enter the
secular priesthood. No one was surprised when a
brief month after his ordination he was named at the
beginning of the second college term in February,
professor of philosophy in the new college of the
diocese of New York which had been opened at
Nyack on the Hudson. It was very probably fortunate for him and his career that the college was
destroyed by fire in its first year, for otherwise he
would almost surely have continued in the arduous
duties of professor of philosophy for some years at

least. His health was not such as would permit him
to give himself at that time to work of this character. There was serious danger after his dozen
of years of college and his devotion to his studies of
an almost inevitable breakdown. This would probably have been rather serious in character, for the
men of that time, knowing how much their services
were needed, did not give up until they could not
possibly go on and the result might have been very
definitely harmful for his future work and career,
but providentially he was spared that danger.

After the fire Father McCloskey asked permission to travel in Europe in order to prepare himself
for further teaching work. No one knew better
than he how much he lacked to make him a good
teacher. As it would be some considerable time
before the college could be reopened, he was given
permission to spend a year or more in Europe and
his leave of absence lengthened itself out to three
years and he had a magnificent chance, which was
taken very well, to secure all the advantages of a
European tour and particularly of a prolonged residence in Rome.

He kept a diary of this trip which has served
to show succeeding generations how much he valued
the opportunities that were thus afforded them,
though at the same time it makes very clear how

much his own gentle scholarliness was recognized and his character appreciated by men who were themselves leaders of thought at that time. It is interesting, for instance, to realize that this young man of twenty-five who had the advantage only of what would be called in all candor a "backwoods education" in America, made lifelong friends during his stay in Rome of such prominent Church dignitaries as Cardinals Fesch and Weld.

Above all, his diary serves to reveal his own discernment of talent and character, for some of those with whom he was brought in contact in his years in Rome were those who were not only to be raised to the dignity of cardinal later in life, such men as Reisach, Angelo Mai, Mezzofanti, Wiseman and Cullen, but who were to be looked upon as the leading churchmen and scholars of their generation. There must have been something very precious in the personality of this young man from America to have attracted the attention of these distinguished churchmen. The very fact that he came to know them and admire them was of itself the best portent of the distinction which he himself was to reach later in life. His Roman experience was indeed of the greatest value to him because bringing him in touch with these great churchmen it prepared his mind and heart and soul for his future work in

America. In the course of his lifetime the American republic was to accumulate a population larger than any of the European countries except Russia and was to take her place among the major nations of the earth. To have the advantage of the future years of a man thus brought in contact with the greatest churchmen of his generation was indeed to be of the most signal benefit to the American Church.

The delicacy of his health would not permit the young priest to become a formal student in any of the colleges in Rome, but he took up his residence in the monastery of the Theatines at San Andrea del Valle was registered as a special student of the Gregorian University conducted by the Jesuits. Here he sat under such learned professors as Fathers Perrone and Manera, men who carried out admirably the traditions of the finest days of Jesuit teaching in the Gregorian University. The Jesuits had been suppressed in 1773 and the "new society" as it was still called was as yet scarcely a generation away from the restoration but already it was demonstrating very clearly that the best traditions of the old society were living on again after the resurrection. Father McCloskey proceeded to take advantage of this to the fullest extent possible for him.

While his health did not permit hard study the

necessity for gentle exercise in the open air took him
out every day to view the monuments of Rome until
he became intimately familiar with all the great
landmarks of the city. The traditional culture of
Rome with its long years of history and its memorials of the Republic, of the Empire, of the classic
writers and the great emperors, of the Fathers of
the Church, of the Middle Ages, and finally of the
Renaissance, were everywhere around him there and
influenced him deeply. The result of these fortunate
opportunities almost thrust upon him was that he
became very literally a man of fine culture and of
profound sympathy with all the great movements
of thought in history. He thoroughly appreciated
the chances for that education higher than most
people could possibly secure that were thus afforded
him. He missed none of them. He probably
realized that only to few men is given the opportunity thus afforded him to secure breadth and depth
of education in what so well deserve to be called
the humanities.

Every day had its task and each new setting sun
found him knowing a little more of this wonderful
old city which contains in a palimpsest, so many of
the phases of the history of human development.
Such expressions might seem to be merely bits of
more or less imaginative trimming introduced by a

biographer but he himself wrote in a letter to a friend, "Each day affords new sources of pleasure and an intellectual banquet of which one can never partake to satiety." He realized, moreover, how fortunate he was in having had his long years of classical and ecclesiastical training at "The Mountain," which enabled him to appreciate all this, for in writing to that same friend he said, "What cannot one enjoy who comes to this great classic and holy city with a mind prepared to appreciate its historic and religious charms?"

After more than two years spent in Rome in this gloriously educational way, Father McCloskey spent the most of a third year in travel through Italy, France, Germany, Belgium, England and Ireland. He had the chance in the forties of the nineteenth century to make what they used to call in the eighteenth century the "grand tour," which university students, especially in England, were expected to make on the Continent as a sort of graduate work. We are inclined to think in our day of graduate work as a comparatively modern invention but nothing, so far as I know, that we have at the present time, could possibly compare in significance with a year or more of travel on the Continent, interested in art and architecture, in the arts and crafts, and in the peoples and their ways, which so many eighteenth-century students enjoyed. It must have been of the greatest broadening influence of mind and must have represented a real culmination of education. The fact that travel was ever so much slower than at the present time was a decided advantage. People could not be whisked from large city to large city, seeing scarcely anything of points along the way, but had to stop at many of the smaller places overnight at least and often for some days and saw the country leisurely and were likely to come in intimate contact with the typically national ways and not merely with the tourist customs of certain larger cities.

The period during which Father McCloskey was in Rome and on his travels in Europe was a very precious one for the Church. The French Revolution had very seriously disturbed men's minds and led a great many of them away from their loyalty to the Church. France, the eldest daughter of the Church, so far from being the representative Catholic country had become the home of rationalism and atheism, and with her religious dispersed, her monasteries suppressed, many of her bishops banished when not guillotined, it seemed almost impossible that France should ever again be the home of a great Catholic people. To many outside the Church it seemed as though Napoleon's imprisonment of the

Pope meant the death knell of the power of the papacy and the end of world influence for the Catholic Church for all time.   At the beginning of the nineteenth century the Catholic Church seemed almost a thing of the past still hanging on to life but inevitably dying and surely destined to a very proximate decadence that made any future greatness out of the question and any prospective influence outside of the Latin countries, particularly, almost utterly visionary.

Of the Latin countries Spain was so decadent that her Catholicity could not be presumed to have any influence outside of that country.   The Napoleonic troubles had precipitated all sorts of unfortunate tendencies which, on the background of the French Revolution, seemed to assure the sapping of faith in Church life.   Spain was gradually losing her South American colonies and it seemed only a question of time until the revolutionary habit acquired by the Spanish and Portuguese Americans would do away with any influence the Catholic hierarchy might have. Germany was hopelessly Protestant and gradually becoming rationalistic.   Austria still clung to the Church but consisted of such disparate elements under its imperialistic government that it seemed destined to approaching dissolution and with it would disappear the one important European power that still gave its unquestioning adhesion to the Pope.   Italy was helplessly divided into smaller political units, the important northern portion under hopeless Austrian tyranny.   England, during the eighteenth century, had lost most of its religious faith and its Anglican Church life was in sad decadence.   While there was some initiative left in the non-Conformists they were drifting farther and farther away from anything like Catholicity.

Toward the end of the first quarter of the nineteenth century the reaction toward the Catholic Church began very strongly.   The return of the monarchy and the reëstablishment of the French hierarchy revealed a readiness on the part of the French people to take up Catholicity once more in a way that could scarcely have been believed.   Then came the rise of a group of brilliant Frenchmen who accomplished wonders in touching the hearts and souls as well as the minds of the Frenchmen of the rising generation.   I need only mention such names as Montalembert, Lacordaire, the unfortunate Lamennais and Ozanam, all of whom, with the exception of Lamennais, were within ten years of the age of Father McCloskey, to give some idea of the wind of the spirit that was abroad among his contemporaries, and how likely he was to be touched by it not only during his time abroad but afterwards

because of familiarity with European conditions.
Montalembert's *St. Elizabeth of Hungary,* which
was the leading factor of a great literary revival of
understanding of the Middle Ages, was published
while Father McCloskey was abroad. It was precious to be alive but it was glorious to be young and
with one's heart deeply immersed in the interests of
the Catholic Church at that time.

The French reaction awakened the English across
the Channel and brought about the Oxford movement, the first deep stirrings of which must have
been already very noticeable during the time while
Father McCloskey was in England and Ireland.
Newman's "Lead Kindly Light" was written just
before Father McCloskey left America but was
coming into attention during his stay over there.
The "Tracts for the Times" were just attracting
very wide attention during the years while Father
McCloskey was in Europe. His friend, Professor
Wiseman, was made bishop *in partibus* with the
English mission in prospect in 1840, that is within a
very few years after Father McCloskey returned.
It is easy to understand how deeply he was pene-
trated by the feeling that there was a great new
future for the Catholic Church just ahead and that
nowhere might this be looked for as more likely to
reap a very great success than in his own native

country, America, where the freedom of religion
guaranteed by the Constitution had already proved
so favorable for the establishment of the hierarchy
and the organization of the Church free from political or governmental influences of any kind. It was
in this temper of mind that Father McCloskey must
have returned to America to take up his work in
the ministry.

Cardinal Farley, in his *Life of Cardinal McCloskey,* has dwelt on the high points of this reaction so
well that it would be presumptuous for any one else
to try to tell the story, especially in the amount of
space that can be given to it in a sketch of this kind.
He said, "A spirit of renewed loyalty to the Church
was strongly moving European centres of thought.
Lacordaire had in 1835 begun his Notre Dame
'Conferences,' which commanded the attention of all
France and drew around his pulpit the skeptical
youth of Paris; Dr. Wiseman, as rector of the English College in Rome, was giving his 'Lectures on
the Connexion between Science and Revealed Religion,' which gained him the ear of all England;
Döllinger by the first and second parts of his *History
of the Church,* Görres by his *Christian Mysticism,*
and Möhler by his *Symbolism* had begun to fix the
attention of Germany on the power of the Church
to hold men of ability. The Catholic Movement

under Newman had begun at Oxford; Montalembert had succeeded in forming a Catholic party in France, with himself as president. Father McCloskey's intimate knowledge of all these forces, focussed as they were in the Eternal City, gave him ever after a broader and more intelligent interest in the affairs of the Church, especially in Europe, and made his forecast of things singularly accurate in after life."

All this fine opportunity came to Father McCloskey in the very impressionable years just under and over twenty-five and when he had just been prepared by years of classical study to take in new impressions. Those who knew him in after life intimately and who appreciated how interesting a conversationalist he was and how broad were his sympathies for all European questions, had brought home to them the effect of this graduate European work. He knew at first hand a great many things that enabled him to understand movements that occurred in Europe, the real significance of which would be quite hidden from those who had not had opportunity for his experience. I doubt if more than a very few men of his day here in the United States, a dozen or a score at most, and those mainly who had had diplomatic opportunities in Europe, were so broadly and culturally educated as Father

McCloskey on his return. Quite needless to say the effect of this education was noteworthy all during his life and made him a very enjoyable companion for those who were brought closely in touch with him. There was crying need for such a man in the American Church and Father McCloskey came almost as a direct response to the unuttered, because as yet unrecognized, demand for refinement and culture as well as zeal and loyalty among the Catholic clergy in the United States.

From the happy, satisfying, scholarly period of Roman absorption of the humanities, with all the satisfaction of mind and heart that that implied for a man of his gentle studious character, Father McCloskey, on his return to America, was transferred to a position that at once demanded all the power of character, yet of sympathy for others, of which he was possessed. Though he had had no experience as a pastor and was after all well under thirty years of age, when most men are considered to be scarcely mature enough for a responsible administrative position, he was made the parish priest of one of the most important parishes in the archdiocese of New York, that of St. Joseph's, on lower Sixth Avenue. If the parish had been in perfectly normal condition the burden that it imposed would have been only trying because of the

immense number of practical details which had to
be overseen, as a substitute for the academic occupations which for so long had been the principal
occupation of Father McCloskey's mind. The
parish was as a matter of fact, however, very far
from being in a normal condition. Indeed it could
not have been much worse and the young studious-
minded pastor was rudely thrust upon some very
delicate and important problems.

Old St. Joseph's parish was at the time one of
the strongholds in New York of that series of
abuses in the history of the American Church in the
first half of the nineteenth century known as trus-
teeism. This was a form of church government
which had gradually arisen in America in the early
days of Catholicism in the United States partly as
the result of the spirit of independence which re-
publican institutions fostered among the citizens
and partly because of the example set in the matter
by the status of other churches in which this form
of government was the rule. In this form of church
government the trustees were elected by the church
congregation. They held the church property in
their names, they paid the pastor's salary and also
that of his assistants, they had the decision with
regard to church affairs and property extension.
In a word all the financial arrangements of the

church devolved on them, leaving to the pastor only the spiritual duties of the care for his flock. It is not surprising that under the circumstances the trustees expected to have certain rights of final judgment with regard to the pastor they should have and the conditions of his pastorate, and especially the termination of it if he did not fit in with their ideas of what a pastor should be, or if on the other hand it seemed good to the bishop for appropriate reasons to transfer the pastor to some other charge.

The result of this situation was the development of a very definite tendency to dictate not only to the pastor but also to the bishop in matters distinctly belonging to their spheres of influence, and it is not surprising that before long a great many abuses crept in. This anomalous condition so far as church government in the Catholic Church is concerned had been allowed to grow up in the early days because of the unsettled church conditions in this country. Very often a group of people to whom no pastor had been assigned as yet, nor could be because of the scarcity of priests, came together and organized a congregation, assessing themselves for the acquisition of the church property and the building of the church and inviting the bishop to supply them with a priest as soon as and as far as that might be feasible. Good work begun out of the purest of Christian zeal however sometimes degenerated into very personal jealousy and the formation of cliques in the congregation led to unfortunate divisions and to no little insubordination to Church authority.

St. Joseph's afforded a striking example of the extent to which abuses might be carried in connection with this system of trusteeship. When Father McCloskey was appointed pastor of the church the trustees of St. Joseph's refused to receive him, demanding to have a pastor of their own choice instead of this young man who had had no experience as a pastor and whose life had been spent in academic obscurity up to this time. When they were told that the bishop must have the right to appoint the pastor and that they must receive the one he had chosen for them, a great many of them refused to attend church. Many of the members of the congregation gave up their pews and as Father McCloskey used to tell, when later on he was cardinal, Sunday after Sunday for many months he preached to almost empty benches. It is easy to understand what a serious disappointment at the beginning of his practical ministry it must have been for this young priest, full of the spirit of the Church, after his years at Rome to find that sometimes there were not a dozen of persons in the church on Sunday. As their pastor he was responsible for the souls of his congregation and it must have been the source of many an anxious moment to have him brought face to face, week after week, with the bitter obstinacy of his flock. Personally he had nothing to do with the unfortunate state of affairs except in so far as his shortcomings as a young man with no experience made him unacceptable to the trustees. He was sent by the bishop and and must do his work as best he could, but it was deeply discouraging to have no chance to influence his flock. His feelings would be very different from those of the pastors in non-Catholic churches for he knew that the members of his congregation were well aware that the violation of the Church rule with regard to attendance at Mass on Sundays made them seriously at fault before the bar of their own consciences. Their attendance at church was not a voluntary but a necessary duty as Catholics.

The church finances were entirely in the hands of the trustees and they refused to pay him a salary. This made the question of his support a rather difficult matter. The board of trustees resented particularly that this young, delicate priest, who looked so much younger even than his years, should have been sent to them as their pastor, for they considered themselves, and not without reason, as the representatives of one of the most important parishes in the diocese. Many invidious remarks were made and most of them of course were carried to the object of them, about his lack of suitability or usefulness for his position. While the "crime of being a young man" is not a serious one and is quite naturally wiped out by the course of time itself, this is one of the objections to his activities that is likely to touch a young man's feelings almost more than anything else. Remarks were even made for the benefit of the pastor—and of course carried to him —in which the trustees went so far as to say that his eloquent and elaborate sermons, which proved so interesting to the few who heard them that the fame of them went abroad throughout the parish, were not really composed by the young man himself but by some older and abler head in compliance with the determined policy of the bishop to impose this young man on them.

Father McCloskey was young in years and younger in experience and even more youthful in appearance, but he had the tact and discretion that an older man might envy. To all these rumors he turned a deaf ear and was as if he had heard nothing so far as any sign of even the slightest irritation as a consequence of them was concerned. He never made even the most distant of passing allusions to all that he heard not only in his church announcements but even in his conversation with members of his congregation. Talebearers were not welcomed and soon stopped coming. He was careful to show no sign in private conversation of any disturbance of feeling on his part. He wanted to be the good shepherd of all his flock and he was, if anything, more kind to the erring ones than to the others. Indeed, that was the only sign that they could have had that he knew of some of their activities in opposition and the expressions they used concerning him. Most of his flock were Irish and when in danger of death the pastor was sent for and always came promptly. Over and over again when affliction came to those who had been most obstinate in their opposition, he proved to be the gentlest and kindliest of *sogarths* in their regard. It required patience of a high order and persistence in what was really a saintly policy but gradually he won and even the most obdurate of his opponents came to recognize that their youthful-looking pastor was a real father in God to them and a Christian nobleman whose thought was all for them and not for himself.

St. Francis de Sales said that a drop of honey draws more flies than a barrel of vinegar and that saying was exemplified very strikingly in old St. Joseph's parish in regard to their gentle, sweetly-tempered young pastor. Slight and frail though he was in physical make-up, he was known by all those who were best acquainted with him for his determination of character and he persisted unremittingly in his work of winning over especially the recalcitrant members of his flock by his gentleness and patience. Those who knew Father McCloskey best were sure that he would win the contest with his parishioners because they knew that there was literally no end to his abiding persistence of character in doing whatever he had made up his mind was the right thing. A college companion at Emmitsburg who had known him very well for many years summed up the whole situation at St. Joseph's and the inevitable outcome of it when he said succinctly, but very strikingly, "Father McCloskey will not fight but he will conquer." The pastor set a magnificent example of that charity which is kind and patient and mild and gentle and long-suffering and which seeketh not its own and that has never been known to fail ultimately in its purpose of winning souls to the right.

Those who were most bitterly opposed to him when he first came to St. Joseph's became his firmest supporters in the course of time and the young

priest, after even a few years, came to be looked
up to by his large flock with a reverence that is
usually only accorded to the man whom the snows of
years have crowned and whom a series of generations of parishioners have had brought close to
them at all the precious crises of family life—deaths
and births and marriages—that make the relations
between the pastor and his people so intimate as to
represent spiritual affinities which exceed in significance even the natural ties of relationship. Toward
the end of his life when Cardinal Archbishop of
New York and when his long experience of humanity would seem to have afforded him many
opportunities for happiness in the accomplishment
of great work in the hierarchy, Cardinal McCloskey
used to say that the years which followed those
first severe trials at old St. Joseph's, when it seemed
for a time as though he might be unsuited for the
practical ministry of the Church, were actually the
happiest of his life. His flock had tried him as
by fire but his winning of them over had made him
realize the wonderful power that the Church has
over the hearts of the people and how much can be
accomplished by its ministrations better than all his
years of study and even his knowledge of the history
of the Church for nearly 2,000 years as it had been
brought home to him in Rome.

With his success as a pastor at St. Joseph's, making it very clear how valuable a man Father McCloskey would make in the fulfillment of pastoral duties, his religious superiors had not forgotten that Father McCloskey was also one of the best-educated men in the diocese with a well-stored mind and an enthusiasm for teaching that would make him more valuable in college work than probably in any other position. Though he was only thirty-one years of age, Father McCloskey was selected by Bishop Hughes as the first president of St. John's College, Fordham. After the fire at Nyack, Fordham had been chosen as the site of the diocesan college which Bishop Hughes wished to create. The foundation there has continued ever since and has now become Fordham University under the Jesuits, with many thousands of students, the *alma mater* of a large number of men who have occupied positions of influence in Church and State during the nineteenth and twentieth centuries.

It is a sign of what a scarcity of laborers there was in the field that even when he became president of the new college Father McCloskey still retained his pastorate at St. Joseph's, though almost needless to say, travel from lower Sixth Avenue out to Fordham, some ten miles, was a rather slow process in those days and this of itself must have made the new position rather time-taking and strenuous, especially during winter weather.

His interest in scholarship made him the most suitable for that position and his love of young folks, and especially of boys, made him an ideal rector, as he was called in those days, for the new college. He did much in its earliest years to assure the success of the institution. All his life he continued to maintain a very special interest in it so that Fordham came to be looked upon as one of the leading Catholic colleges of the country.

Three years after Father McCloskey's appointment to the rectorship of Fordham, when Bishop Hughes asked for an assistant bishop to help him bear some of his immense diocesan burdens, Pope Gregory XVI selected Father McCloskey for the position, and on March 10, 1844, he was consecrated Bishop of Axiere and Coadjutor of New York with the right of succession. At this time the diocese of New York included the whole state of New York and most of New Jersey. In those days of extremely difficult travel it is easy to understand what a difficult problem was before the Bishop of New York in the effort to care for his flock. With two bishops that work would be divided, while yet for each of them the proper visitation of the diocese remained an almost impossible task. The perilous

state of the primitive roads of that time in con-
junction with horse travel made it almost impossible
to fulfill all the duties which the bishops felt incumbent upon them. Those problems and tasks were
increasing all the time. The population was growing rapidly and this was adding to the difficulties.
Bishop McCloskey gave himself to his new duties
whole-heartedly and must have been of immense
assistance to Bishop Hughes. The steady immigration from Ireland was increasing the number of
their flock by leaps and bounds so that the New
York diocese was probably growing more rapidly
than any other diocese in the Catholic world at that
time.

In 1847, the steady growth of the Church in New
York State necessitated the division of the New
York diocese into three dioceses, the two new Sees
being located at Albany and Buffalo. Bishop Mc-
Closkey had been installed as Coadjutor Bishop of
New York, which was now become the most important diocese in the United States. He had the
right of succession in that great diocese and undoubtedly any insistence on his part on this right
would have secured him in this position. It is an
index of his unselfish character, however, and of his
earnest wish to devote himself to what he thought
best for the Church that he resigned his coadjutor-

ship of New York to take up the organization of the
new diocese of Albany, May 21, 1847. Here he
had nearly half the state of New York in area
under his jurisdiction in a diocese extending over
30,000 square miles. In the whole region there
were less than twenty-five churches and but twenty-
four priests. The Catholics who had to be served
by these were widely scattered, most of them poor
working people, many of them immigrants just getting settled in the country, and they numbered sixty
thousand. The conditions particularly in the winter
time, when the temperature was often thirty or more
degrees below zero in the northern part of the state
in what was then called the North Woods, now the
Adirondacks, made the tasks of the priests extremely
difficult.

What Bishop McCloskey achieved in Albany in
what must have often seemed to him the most discouraging circumstances and in the midst of physical
labors and hardships of travel under the most rigor-
ous weather conditions, all of which seemed destined
inevitably to break down his frail frame before his
appointed time, exemplified very well the spirit of
the man, his utter forgetfulness of himself, and his
life purpose of devoting himself to the benefit of
others. It was wonderful how much he was able
to accomplish. His preëminent success, for he left a

name that is in benediction in Albany ever since—
and he organized that diocese very wonderfully
—demonstrated beyond peradventure, that he was
indeed the man for higher positions, a worthy
churchman with his heart in his work.

His successor, Cardinal Farley, said of him and
his work in Albany: "After seventeen years of his
administration of Albany he left behind as a result
a noble cathedral, eighty-four priests, one hundred
and thirteen churches, eight chapels, forty-four
minor stations, eighty-five missionaries, three academies for boys, one for girls, six orphan asylums,
fifteen parochial schools, and St. Joseph's Provincial Seminary, Troy, which he, with Archbishop
Hughes, was largely instrumental in securing and
equipping. He also introduced into the diocese several religious communities, amongst others, the
Augustinians, the Jesuits, the Franciscans, the Capu-
chins, and Oblates. For the care of the young girls
under his charge, he provided by inviting the Religious of the Sacred Heart to Kenwood-on-the-Hud-
son; the Sisters of Charity, the Sisters of Mercy and
the Sisters of St. Joseph; and for the boys the
Christian Brothers were also introduced."

In January, 1864, John Hughes, who in 1842,
had become the Bishop, and in 1847 the first Arch-

bishop of New York, died, and the question of his successor came to be one of the most important problems for the Catholic Church in America. Though Baltimore was the primatial see it was felt that New York, as the largest city in the country, should have as its archbishop the most representative clergyman of the time. Archbishop Hughes' personality had raised the Archiepiscopal See of New York to a very high place of public esteem in the United States. In his controversy with Breckenridge he had attracted countrywide attention. The diplomatic mission which Lincoln had seen fit to confide to him in order to dissipate, if possible, some of the danger that there seemed to be of European states combining to recognize the belligerency of the Confederacy and thus be free to supply them with munitions of war and other needed materials, had made the Archbishop of New York a power in the country. His magnificent administration of his great archdiocese and especially what he had accomplished in order to bring under his jurisdiction in formal way and provide proper church accommodations for the immense number of immigrants who after the famine found their way into New York, added to his prestige and was recognized particularly by the Church authorities. All this had made his archdiocese one of the largest in the point of membership in the Church anywhere in the Catholic world.

Here was a post that almost any man might be glad to be chosen for, since it represented practically the most important position in the Catholic Church in America. A great many people were of the opinion that the logical appointee for the Archiepiscopal See of New York was Bishop McCloskey of Albany. He had already been named as the coadjutor bishop with the right of succession to that see and he had resigned that right solely in order to take on his shoulders the heavy burden of organizing the new diocese of Albany. It seemed as though a man who had thus given up his claim to this lofty post just because he saw the opportunity for hard work for the Church should now have accorded to him the high dignity voluntarily foregone but that called loudly for him after the death of Archbishop Hughes.

Bishop McCloskey himself seemed to be almost the only one who did not have that feeling. He had spent years, and as he felt his best forces, in accomplishing the organization of the Albany diocese. In spite of the practically universal call of the priests and people of the archdiocese as well as the formally expressed wish of the bishops of the country, Bishop McCloskey felt that he should not be asked to assume the burden of the archbishopric no matter how enviable the dignity might be. He was as yet only fifty-four years of age, but he had never been strong and he feared the giving out of his powers and he felt that some younger, more active and more capable man than himself should be promoted to the archbishopric.

For those who are inclined to think that surely ambition must rule the lives of clergy as it does those of laymen, and that the opportunity to secure a high dignity of this kind must certainly break down any feelings of humility a man may entertain, Bishop McCloskey's conduct on this occasion should prove illuminating. While human motives must in his case, as in that of other men, have had a very strong appeal, so far from being allowed to rule his conduct, they were thoroughly suppressed and the bishop himself made every effort to prevent his advancement to the post that seemed so well worth while coveting. There is a letter from the Bishop of Albany written to Cardinal Reisach, who was at the moment one of the most influential members of the Congregation of Propaganda at Rome, which shows how Bishop McCloskey tried to avert the coming of the dignity that seemed to be already looming over him. At that time the United States was so far as its Church status was concerned a missionary country directly under the control of Propaganda. The officials of that Congregation had more to do with the naming of the new Archbishop of New York than any one else, for while the Pope actually named the appointee he did not do so without consultation with Propaganda and almost invariably chose the one suggested by them.

It is evident that this letter of Bishop McCloskey's was written in the hope and with the deliberate purpose that he would be able to counteract any influences that might possibly be at work in Rome for his appointment as archbishop. He knew how much that appointment was desired for him over here in America, though of course his priests and people of Albany were very much disturbed over the thought of losing their beloved prelate. Bishop McCloskey was confident that his letter would dispel any tendencies there might be to transfer him to New York. After reading that letter there can be no possible doubt that the Bishop of Albany was eminently sincere in his desire to be allowed to remain in his beloved diocese of Albany where his comparative obscurity was the surest warrant of peace and happiness for himself. Behind this motive that might well have been considered selfish there were other and stronger motives that impelled him in the line of conduct that he adopted. He feared that he would not be able to fill the higher position properly and he felt sure that there were others who could do ever so much better for the Church than he could possibly hope to do and his one idea was that the Church of Christ should benefit as much as possible and that, above all, his feelings should not be considered in the matter nor be allowed to stand in the way of the greater glory of God as he feared that they might.

Bishop McCloskey wrote to Cardinal Reisach, the dear personal friend of his years at Rome who would understand, if anybody could, how candid and open of soul the Bishop of Albany was in his expression—"I write to implore your Eminence in case there should be any danger of my appointment or of my being transferred from Albany to New York, to aid me in preventing it, and to save me from the humiliation and misery of being placed in a position for the duties and responsibilities of which I feel myself both physically and morally unequal and unfit. After having been appointed and consecrated coadjutor of the Bishop of New York, with the right of succession, I resigned both coadjutorship and right of succession to come to Albany. I then resolved, and still hold to the resolution, that, as far as it depended on any free will or consent of my own, I should never again return to New York.

Having been relieved from the prospect of succession, I never thought of afterwards aspiring or being called to it. I speak only from the deepest sincerity of heart and from the strongest conviction of conscience when I say that I possess neither the learning, nor prudence, nor energy, nor firmness, nor bodily health or strength which are requisite for such an arduous and highly responsible office as that of Archbishop of New York. I recoil from the very thought of it with shuddering, and I do most humbly trust that such a crushing load will not be placed upon my weak and unworthy shoulders."

Fortunately for us we have a commentary upon this letter from one who knew Bishop McCloskey very well and whose own experience in life was such as to make his opinion of very great weight. Cardinal Farley, the second successor of Cardinal McCloskey in the archbishopric of New York and the second cardinal to occupy that See, in writing a sketch of Cardinal McCloskey for the Catholic Encyclopedia quotes the letter, or at least those portions of it which we have given, and says of it— "This soul revealing letter tells that the Church still has within her hierachy men of the stamp of Chrysostom, Basil and Gregory Nazianzen, men who strained every nerve to avoid honors as much as men of the world strive for them."

In spite of the heavy burden thus placed on his frailty which in his declining years became more noticeable than it had been in the early days, Cardinal McCloskey lived on to the ripe age of seventy-five. It has often been noted that small thin men are, barring accidents, likely to have a longer lease of life than their more sturdy brethren. It has been suggested that their souls have to inform less matter and that what they lose in intensity of material life they gain in its extension. It is surprising how often these small thin men prove to be capable of doing demanding work in positions of great responsibility and yet live on well beyond the psalmist's limit.

It is very probable that at no time during life did Cardinal McCloskey feel that there was any guarantee of prolongation of existence for him for any lengthy period. Those who were near him said that they often had the feeling that when he made decisions looking to the future they were almost invariably made with that delicate conscientiousness that would take possession particularly of a man who felt that life might have ended for him before the last effects of this decision of his would be felt. There is nothing like such a feeling to make a man unselfish and thoughtful only of duty as he sees it.

During my years as a student at Fordham in the

early eighties, I had the pleasure of seeing the good
Cardinal Archbishop of New York of that time on
a number of occasions. I had the privilege of being
introduced to him on the occasion of our graduation.
The fact that he had been the first president of the
original college located at Fordham always gave
him a fatherly feeling with regard to the institution
and he seemed at his best among us at commencement time. There were many memorials at Fordham that must have brought back to him the days
of his presidency there. The old Rose Hill Manor,
still used as the administration building (it is even
yet in use), the previous manor house used as an
infirmary, with the tradition that it had been Washington's headquarters and others of the older buildings, greeted him from the old times.

The gentle quiet of his ways, the charm of his
personality, the sweetness of his voice, all made one
feel that here, indeed, was a most precious character. He was interested particularly in the younger
boys and they represented a large part of the students in those days, for we had them from the
earliest preparatory classes, studying even the elements. The cardinal made it a point to get in
touch with the youngest among them and greet them
affectionately. Any excuse was sufficient to make
him single out one of the very young boys for atten-

tion and when a little group would gather round him it was easy to see how intensely pleased he was among them. One could not help but have the feeling that, like his Divine Master, nothing pleased him more than to be able to say, "Permit little children to come unto Me and prevent them not." He himself retained always a simplicity of character that made the younger folks take to him and find real pleasure in his visit to them.

Archbishop McCloskey attended the Vatican Council (1871) at all its sessions and took a prominent part in its proceedings. He was a member of one of the most important commissions, that on discipline, and cardinals who came to know him at that time learned to appreciate his prudence and his wisdom. Indeed, it was during his stay in Rome for the Vatican Council that he made the definite impression upon the ecclesiastical authorities in the capital of Christendom which led to his elevation to the cardinalate. It has sometimes been said that he was opposed to the definition of the infallibility of the Pope which was the principal act of this Council, but those who recall his attitude are very emphatic in the declaration that what he opposed was the opportuneness of the definition at that moment. This was an opinion shared by many of the members of the Council and particularly by a number of

the American members of the hierarchy who were
at the Council. The fact that within four years he
was made a cardinal is of itself the best demonstration of the fact that whatever his position with
regard to infallibility was, it was felt that it was
dictated by the sincerest motives.

The reception of the news that he had been made
cardinal was received in this country with universal
applause not only from Catholics but also from
Protestants. This was probably the first piece of
Catholic news, especially originating in Rome, to be
so welcomed generally by our people. Americans
felt that the honor conferred on the Archbishop of
New York accrued also to the prestige of the United
States itself as a whole. There were, as was quite
inevitable, some mutterings of bigotry and intolerance, but liberal-minded Protestants, as well as
Catholics, felt that this high dignity had been conferred on a very worthy representative of American
institutions and the first long step on the pathway
away from old-time prejudice was taken. There
were many old-fashioned Catholics who were quite
sure that an appointment of this kind from the Pope,
blazoned forth in all the papers of the country,
would surely be the signal for an outburst of bigotry
and intolerance such as had followed the reëstablishment of the Catholic hierarchy in England a

quarter of a century before, but as Cardinal Farley said, in his sketch of Cardinal McCloskey, the appointment actually proved "the proverbial wisdom of Rome" in its relations with even distant countries. Cardinal McCloskey's investiture took place in the old cathedral on Mott Street, April 27, 1875. The biretta was conferred by Archbishop Bailey, of Baltimore, who had been made delegate of the Apostolic See for this purpose.

The finishing of St. Patrick's Cathedral, which had been begun by his great predecessor, Archbishop Hughes, was delayed during the war, for every effort was concentrated on the great struggle between North and South. It was some years after the war before the work could be carried on with the industry that was desirable. While New York had a very large number of Catholics, a great many of them were poor and the accumulation of funds for the cathedral was slow. The medieval cathedrals, which are such magnificent structures to have been constructed in the small towns in which so often they were situated, were built by the labor of the people themselves to a very great extent and by the small contributions of those who had very little to spare, but who were willing to make sacrifices for the sake of a church worthy, as far as possible, of Emmanuel. St. Patrick's Cathedral was largely

built by similar small contributions. The humorous
remark of the Irish servant girl, who said to her
friend, "Sure it's my tin cints and your tin cints that
has helped to build this great church," had much
more of truth than of humor in it, or rather the
humor was due to the truth of it.

This handsome building then, one of the most
beautiful that New York has, and sometimes proclaimed the handsomest ecclesiastical structure on
the continent, as it surely was up to the beginning of
the twentieth century, at least, is owed to the faith
and willing sacrifices of poor people. Cardinal
McCloskey devoted himself to the task of complet-
ing it and nothing was too much for him to do in
order to fulfill this purpose within his lifetime. He
visited Europe several times in order to procure win-
dows and altars for it, taking the best of advice and
securing, especially when the taste of that time is
considered in such matters, very marvelous results.
After all a great change has come over the æsthetic
feelings of all classes during the fifty years that have
elapsed since then. Churches were to a very great
extent up to that time almost hideously obtrusive
in their mere attention to utility and in their accumulation of adventitious and often cheap and tawdry
ornaments. But in St. Patrick's the beauty all came
out in the structure itself and it was a triumph of

old-time Gothic. In order to secure its completion Cardinal McCloskey finally gave everything that he possessed in the world and he had the consolation, on May 25, 1879, of dedicating it to the service of God.

The last notable public appearance of Cardinal McCloskey was on the occasion of the celebration of the fiftieth anniversary of his ordination, January 12, 1884. In reply to the addresses on that day he contrasted the scene of his ordination with that of this fiftieth anniversary. At the first there were a bishop, two priests and a few people in the church. Now the sanctuary was "filled with the bishops of my province and the faithful clergy of my diocese and the great cathedral is crowded to overflowing with my devoted people." In his humility he deprecated the praises that had been lavished on him by those who spoke on the occasion and he declared "with regard to the promotions that have followed one after another, I can only say that not one of them was ever sought by me."

The last public act of Cardinal McCloskey is one for which the Church in America, hierarchy, priests and people, cannot but feel deeply grateful to him for all time, for the effect of it continues to be felt in the benefits conferred by a great American institution in Rome. The Italian government, which had taken over the papal property in Rome after the revolution, proceeded to the expropriation of educational properties of various kinds belonging to the Church. Among others even the North American College at Rome, which had been founded by the American hierarchy and was supported by their contributions, though it had been greatly helped by the liberality of the sovereign pontiffs during the time of their temporal sovereignty, was threatened with confiscation by the government. Cardinal McCloskey laid the matter before President Arthur, appealing for the protection of this institution as the property of American citizens. The Secretary of State, Mr. Frelinghuysen, by the direction of the President, brought the question of the American College to the special notice of the Italian government through the American Minister. The college was saved. Nothing else could have happened in strict justice, but in affairs relating to the Church and its property, justice has been almost the last word to have a meaning in a number of European countries even during this generation of ours which plumes itself so heartily on its sense of justice.

Cardinal McCloskey accomplished an immense amount of work that remains as the monument of his life as a prelate. At his death there were well above half a million of Catholics in his archdiocese. During his archbishopric the priests had increased from 150 to 400, the churches and chapels from 85 to 229, the schools and academies had nearly doubled from 53 to 97, and the pupils in Catholic schools from scarcely more than 15,000 to nearly 40,000. He founded the Catholic Protectory which must ever stand as a striking monument of his foresight in making provision for neglected children. Besides, he added largely to the number of institutions of various kinds for the care of the needy poor, hospitals, asylums and homes, as the growing wants of his people demanded. A great many of them were the poorest of the poor immigrants who came to this country in the most absolute need, driven out from Ireland by recurring famines, but who fortunately had in them the ability to rise and the memory of their own period of distress and want to prompt them to help the head of the archdiocese in his work for the needy.

Cardinal McCloskey was, as we have said, one of the most scholarly men of his time. Those who knew him the best, however, thought not so much about his gifts of intellect, though these were unmistakable, as his gifts of the spirit. His successor in both the archbishopric and the cardinalate said of him, "But all these endowments were as nothing compared to the beauty of his soul which was the seat of all those virtues that render a man acceptable before God and dear to his fellow-men. If we had to mention only one trait of character, we should select what perhaps was the most conspicuous, certainly the most edifying—the admirable blending in him of dignity which repelled none, with a sweetness which attracted all, a rare blessing—

Non bene conveniunt nec in una sede morantur Majestas et amor. . . .

"In the soul of Cardinal McCloskey, where Christian virtue had solid roots, they co-existed in a wonderful manner. In him were coupled the majesty of a prince, which inspired no fear, but exacted the reverence of all, with the simplicity and amiableness of a child. Well may we say of him that he was 'Beloved of God and men.' "

JAMES, CARDINAL GIBBONS

Second American Cardinal

"First Citizen of the United States"

OUR second American cardinal was a man who felt supremely thankful over what he considered the very fortunate circumstance—"the luckiest act of my life," as he once said—that he had been born in the United States, though some of his sisters and brothers before and after him in the family had been born in Ireland. For the sake of father's health the Gibbonses, after moving to America from Ireland and settling down for some years in Baltimore, had gone back to the Irish homeland and remained there for some ten years. Cardinal Gibbons was a great American churchman proud of his Americanism above everything else, and his life was devoted to making his fellow citizens better Americans just in so far as his efforts and the influence of his Church, the great historic Church of Christianity, could accomplish that purpose.

A distinguished professor of science in an Ameri-

can university who was a member of the United
States Food Commission in Belgium during the
Great War, told in one of his articles with regard
to the work that was done there, that when he
first met Cardinal Mercier and looked up to his well
above six feet of stature, he said to himself, "Here
is a *man*." A year later, however, when he had
seen how nobly this man could stand in support of
his tottering country like Horace's just man un-
moved in the midst of what seemed a toppling
world, thoughtful meantime for others but not for
himself, and utterly regardless of personal danger,
meeting the great Belgian cardinal once again he
said to himself, "Here is a saint." Those of us
who had the privilege of meeting Cardinal Gibbons
and of knowing him even a little intimately, were
likely to have produced in us a feeling very like
this. Some one has defined a saint as a person
who thinks first of others and only second of himself or herself. This would seem to leave out the
prayers and self-denial that most of us are inclined
to think of as indispensable for sainthood, but any
one who has tried to practice the habit of thinking
first of others and only second of himself, will very
probably find how indispensable the other commonly
accepted attributes of sanctity are. It was as one
forgetful of self and thoughtful of others above

CARDINAL GIBBONS

all, that those who knew Cardinal Gibbons best estimated him and his character.

This seems the language of panegyric rather than of temperate biography, but even a brief sketch of the career of Cardinal Gibbons will, I think, make it clear how well he deserves even such strong expressions as those which were so appropriately used for his great colleague in the cardinalate, the Cardinal Archbishop of Malines.

The future cardinal was born in a small house in the cathedral parish of Baltimore in which in his later years as archbishop and cardinal he was to be one of the most striking figures in the country. There were many vicissitudes of life in between that at once demonstrated and developed his character. His earliest memory was at the age of three being lifted in his mother's arms in order to see Andrew Jackson, President of the United States, pass by. His parents married in Ireland, Thomas Gibbons and Bridget Walsh, had come out to this country to better themselves and after trying Canada and finding the climate too hard, had settled in Baltimore. His father was a clerk in a shipping office but with the responsibilities of arranging the finances of the ships on his shoulders. He was so known for his exact honesty that there was a proverb in Baltimore "honest as Tom Gibbons." When

James was about three his father fell ill with what was probably tuberculosis and it was thought that the air of his native country might benefit him, so he returned there. He lived on for some ten years and his eldest son, the fourth in the family, received his early education in Ireland * and it seems to have been very solid and thorough.

On the death of his father, his mother, far from being prostrated after the long unsuccessful struggle for her husband's life, felt that now she must be both father and mother to her children. She was convinced that the family would have better opportunities for life in America, so she planned their return. She was a brave woman of indomitable character, so that even the crossing of the Atlantic in the winter time in one of the small vessels of that day did not deter her from securing a better environment for her children just as soon as she could. The crossing took eight weeks and they

* Cardinal Gibbons, as every one knew, had a very tender spot in his heart for Ireland and the Irish; though he was proud to have been born in the United States, he felt toward Ireland almost as if it were his native land, because it had been the birthplace of his father and mother. He once called my attention to the fact that the same family names occurred in both our families, for his grandfather on his mother's side had been James Walsh, and his mother's name, like that of mine, was Bridget, and as both families came from County Mayo in Ireland, they were probably of the same stock originally. This undoubtedly made a more confidential status between us on our comparatively rare meetings than would otherwise have been the case. Some of the personal element thus introduced may be reflected in parts of this sketch.

were sorely tried, but within a few days after their landing they were all ready for work in the new country. Recalling their disturbing experiences with the cold in Canada this time they landed and settled in New Orleans. Hard work was necessary for the benefit of the family now and school days were over. But so far was this from preventing real education that as a matter of fact the next few years of hard work for the support of his mother and the family, the future cardinal often said were the most precious years of his development of intellect and of character.

Justice Joseph Daly of the Supreme Court of New York once said to me that he thought the best education that you can give a boy of fourteen or fifteen is to put his widowed mother on his hands to support. If there is anything in that boy it will come out and his love for his mother will help him to develop his powers to the greatest possible extent. That was what happened to Judge Daly himself when after the death of his father, his mother with himself and his brother Augustine moved to New York. They sold papers on the streets, went to school at night, and lifted themselves up to be one of them among the most distinguished jurists in New York, and the other the most successful theatrical producer in the country and almost in the world, without a smirch of any kind on his character. Education is not pouring in but bringing out and young James Gibbons took his courses in this mode of education with a widowed mother to support in New Orleans about the time the Dalys were taking advantage of the same precious mode of training in New York.

James Gibbons proved to have distinct business ability; that fact was soon recognized and his employer placed more and more responsibility on him. He would undoubtedly have made a very successful business man, but when he was just about twenty-one the Paulists, Fathers Hecker, Walworth and Hewitt, gave a mission in New Orleans. After hearing one of Father Walworth's sermons James Gibbons felt himself called to devote himself to the service of God in the Catholic ministry. His younger brother was already making a success in commercial life and was thoroughly capable of supporting the family and so, though mother was loath to part with her eldest boy, with a true Irish mother's heart, she brought herself readily to be reconciled to the idea of giving him to the Church. Cardinal Gibbons' relations to his family continued until the end of his life to be of the warmest. So far from losing him they had found him. All during life he was bound to them by ties stronger than ever because of his devotion to the service of the Lord.

For his studies he was sent up to St. Charles College, located at Ellicott City, not far from Baltimore in Maryland. The difference between travel then and now will probaby be best understood from the fact that it took him sixteen days to make the trip by steamer up the Mississippi and the Ohio and across country from Wheeling to Baltimore, which as he said afterwards now takes scarcely twice sixteen hours. He was very successful in his studies in St. Charles and came to be looked up to as a model student. His education in Ireland had been so thorough though it might have been considered narrow by those in the modern time, who seem to think that breadth and superficiality of interests can make up for depth and thoroughness, that in two years he was able to complete the college course considered necessary at that time as preparation for the theological seminary. He himself would have preferred to stay at St. Charles longer for he was more hungry for knowledge than ambitious for rapid promotion in his life's work. He was persuaded that the more he learned for the groundwork of his priestly training, the more effective his subsequent work as a priest would be. All his life, however, he remained a student and was very proud to say so, learning something not only every year but every month and almost every day, so that his graduate education made him the rounded scholarly man that he was toward the end of his life.

Like Mt. St. Mary's, Emmitsburg, where our first American cardinal, John McCloskey, went through some of the hard things as a youth that proved the making of his character as an older man, St. Charles College provided opportunity for similar development of character for the second American cardinal.   Only a little comparative study of the two institutions would be needed to show that the conditions which existed as regards washing and bathing facilities and the provision of food were so nearly similar as to be practically identical in effectiveness as discipline for growing youth.

St. Charles College was then housed in a single granite building which had recitation rooms, the professors' rooms and the dormitory of the students all under one roof.   The dormitory was heated by a single large stove and it warmed the students who slept near it pretty well, but those out at the periphery of the room suffered severely from the cold. That first winter, 1855-56, was the coldest in Maryland since 1817, according to the United States Weather Bureau records, and the average temperature for the season was a little below the freezing

point, nearly five degrees below normal. The
thermometer was often at zero and the students
had to break the ice in the water pitchers. For
young Gibbons lately arrived from New Orleans
the change was very hard. No wonder his health
suffered somewhat under it, but he took high rank
in his studies and was a leader in all his classes
during his years there.

After his graduation at St. Charles young Gibbons was allowed to visit his family in New Orleans
and on the way he met for the first time Bishop
Spalding, then in Louisville, later the Archbishop of
Baltimore, who was to give the future cardinal his
first step on the ladder of promotion in the Church.
The young ecclesiastical student seems to have produced a very favorable and lasting impression. He
returned to Baltimore in September to begin his
studies at St. Mary's Theological Seminary. Here
he had the severe discipline of the Sulpicians in
charge of the seminary as a training that was to
prove very precious for life. Fifty years later he
paid a high tribute to what he thought they had
done for him. From his own declaration it is clear
that to the training afforded by the Sulpicians at
St. Mary's it must be considered that the American
Church owes the wonderfully zealous, hard working, self-forgetful clergymen who accomplished so

much for the spread of the Church under the difficult circumstances of those early days. Early in
his seminary career Gibbons suffered from a severe
attack of malaria which discouraged him very much.
Not overstrong naturally this illness seemed as
though it might prove a severe blow to his general
health and strength. His own solicitude was lest
the seminary authorities should find him unsuitable
for the priesthood because of the state of his health.
He felt that that would be the worst misfortune that
could possibly befall him. He was willing to take
all the risks of any possible injury to his health from
the severe discipline to which he was subjected if
he only had the chance to go on.

At St. Charles students and teachers had all been
surprised at the exceptional versatility of his intelligence. This continued to be characteristic of
him all during his student career. At St. Mary's
Seminary the faculty described him as "having exceptional facility in his studies to which he applied
himself with great eagerness." He had come from
St. Charles with the encomium in French *"Bon
esprit; talent,"* of excellent disposition; talented;
and this continued to be the judgment of him. All
during his seminary course he continued to give the
highest satisfaction. He was ordained to the priesthood June 30, 1861.

At the time of his ordination the Civil War was already in progress. Naturally Father Gibbons' sympathies were with the southern people for Marylanders would say that born in Baltimore he was southern by birth and he had lived afterwards in New Orleans, but his better judgment opposed any division of the Union and so he remained a Union man. He took no active side in the controversies so common all around him because as a follower of Christ he felt that it was his duty to do as much good as possible for all those with whom he came in contact. His position was often difficult but it came to be appreciated because of the goodness of heart there was behind it and the readiness to make himself all things to all men.

Father Gibbons' first charge in the ministry was as assistant to Father James Dolan, the beloved pastor of St. Patrick's Church at Fells Point, Baltimore, in a poor, crowded quarter of the city, who was known as "the Apostle of the Point." Father Dolan had built some years before a missionary church out at Canton and six weeks after Father Gibbons' arrival his pastor sent him there to stay, saying in his own very simple, straightforward way, "Canton is a good school for a young priest." Not long after this Father Gibbons was made the regular pastor of this little Church of St. Bridget which he was particularly pleased with because it bore his mother's name. Here he was destined to have his only parish work. There was no rectory and the pastor resided in a few small rooms that formed an addition to one end of the church and were to a great extent without light and ventilation. The church was surrounded by farms and market gardens and only one dwelling was near. That was Mrs. Smyth's, a devoted Catholic, four of whose grandsons became priests. Mrs. Smyth sent him over his first meal on the Saturday evening when he arrived at Canton to begin his ministry. She cared for the housekeeping at the rectory for some time with the assistance of her daughters and sent one of her sons to sleep with him because it was so lonely and even a little dangerous, owing to the isolation of the place.

The Know-Nothing movement had but recently passed. Strange as it may seem, Maryland, where religious tolerance had been first proclaimed, alone of all the United States had been carried by the Know-Nothing party. Bigotry rose almost to frenzy and there was still bitter intolerance in many places. This was followed by the still greater bitterness aroused by the Civil War which divided Baltimore into two hostile camps. The congregation of St. Bridget's was very poor, consisting of laboring men from the Canton copper works and rolling mills with their families and some of the farmer folk. Father Gibbons in his tireless activity as a priest came to know every member of his flock. Many of them remained his personal friends until the end of his life, sure of a smile of recognition whenever they met him.

He was utterly careless of his own comfort and no sacrifice was too much for him if it accrued to the benefit of his flock. He gave up part of his scanty living quarters to provide a room in which meetings of various kinds might be held in connection with the church. This left only a small sleeping room for himself. Sometimes returning at night from pastoral calls he would have to pass through the assembled parishioners saying as he bade them a smiling good night, "I must go to bed now." He even established a parochial school directly above his room and was willing to stand the noise from it in order to have the satisfaction of affording school opportunities for the young of his flock.

No wonder that he attracted the favorable attention of his ecclesiastical superiors. As if he had not work enough, however, he voluntarily assumed charge of St. Lawrence Church on Locust Point, a mile across the Patapsco from St. Bridget's. He had himself rowed across the river every Sunday morning to say Mass there, hear confessions, preach, baptize, and attend sick calls and then recrossed the river to Canton where he celebrated High Mass at half-past ten o'clock and preached again. All this had to be done fasting and it was generally about one o'clock before he broke his fast. There were no conveyances of any kind, his parish cares were wide flung, he learned to take long walks and continued the habit throughout life, and it is probably to this fact that he owed his long life. For a time his parish duties were so demanding that it was feared he was going into a decline which was the euphemism for consumption in those days, but a careful examination by a physician showed that he had no lung trouble and he proceeded to build up and gain strength. His long life attested his constitutional vigor.

He had many trying experiences with intruders of various kinds upon his lonely quarters. He would return to find in possession of them drunken soldiers, insane wanderers, improvident tramps and the like. Sometimes they threatened trouble but yielded to persuasion or well directed energy. The future cardinal came out of the encounters successfully because he was utterly fearless and his moral courage gave him a strength and command of himself that enabled him to tackle successfully much stronger and more robust men.

He had been some four years at Canton in the midst of all this hard work, when an invitation came to him from Archbishop Spalding to give up the pastoral care of his little flock at St. Bridget's and become the archbishop's private secretary. It seemed to him somewhat as though the call involved the turning away from his humble, fruitful field of labor in which he knew he was accomplishing much good for men and women who he felt needed him very much, to take up other easier work for which he was not sure that he was fitted. He used to say himself that the decision to accept the call cost him a sleepless night and that the one reason why he accepted was that given by Father Coskery, the vicar general of the diocese, to whom he went to beg him to exert his influence with the archbishop to allow him to remain at St. Bridget's. The vicar general represented to him that it would be more in accord with his duty as a clergyman for him to leave himself in the hands of his superiors and consider that obedience was better than any sacrifice that he might make. After giving deep consideration to this aspect of the matter the future cardinal accepted the first step in promotion that came to him on his path upwards, writing that he was ready to consider the archbishop's wish as the will of Providence in his regard.

The first important work which came to Father Gibbons as the secretary of Archbishop Spalding was the preliminary organization of the Second Plenary Council of Baltimore which convened in the Cathedral in October, 1866. Archbishop Spalding presided and Father Gibbons as assistant chancellor of the Council managed most of the details. This brought him in contact with the bishops and archbishops of the United States and they learned to appreciate his character, his capacity for work and his intense devotedness to his priestly duties. The Council recommended the formation of a number of new dioceses and one of the new jurisdictions was the Vicariate Apostolic of North Carolina. To this post Father Gibbons though but thirty-two years old and only five years out of the seminary was unanimously nominated by the assembled bishops. He himself was disturbed at the distinction thus conferred on him and feared that he would not be able to carry the burden successfully. When he was consecrated he was known as "the boy bishop." He proceeded to take up his diocesan work in what was probably one of the most unpromising dioceses in the world at that time with a zeal and enthusiasm that amply demonstrated the truth of the fact that the bishops had not been mistaken in their judgment of the youthful secretary of the Council.

North Carolina, never very Catholic in population, had been overrun by the war, had lost many of its inhabitants, and now was in a very disturbed political condition during the reconstruction period. The sudden freeing of the slaves had disorganized labor, the state was dominated by "carpet-baggers," as the politicians from the North who had come down to reconstruct the South were called, and there was political chaos. The new bishop's living quarters were even more modest if possible than those at St. Bridget's. He shared with Father Gross of Wilmington a lean-to built against the rear wall of the church, consisting of four little rooms, two on the ground floor and two upstairs. The floors were bare of even a rug. The furnishings were of the simplest. They slept on cots and ate from a table of rough boards, sometimes preparing their food with their own hands, because they had no funds with which to employ help. Even as it was, they gave away so much in charity of what came to them that they were often almost in want. This was rude preparation for the cardinalate but undoubtedly the opportunities of coming in contact with all classes of men afforded by his episcopal labors in North Carolina made the future cardinal the man who was all things to all men in those precious years at the end of his life when he was probably one of the best known and best loved characters in the United States. There are some things in human life that Providence manages ever so much better than our shortsighted human wisdom can understand until after-vision comes to us.

The bishop made his way through the state over the roads often almost impassable in a rickety wagon of the type locally known as a "democrat." Accompanied by a young priest who drove, or a colored man, they occupied as much of this wagon as was not filled up with packages of sugar, flour, medicines and clothing taken along for the poor families with whom they might stop. The parishioners finally became afraid that the wagon would break down leaving him stranded perhaps twenty miles or more from a habitation and they wanted to get him a new one, but the bishop said, "You can give me the money if you will for the Church but not for a vehicle for my own use."

He traveled throughout the state preaching and teaching, literally following the injunction of Christ "Go and teach" and made a great many friends of all classes, Protestants even more than Catholics because there were so many more of them. He preached in town halls, court-houses, Masonic lodge rooms, even Protestant churches. Sometimes the people were summoned by the Protestant church bell, the Protestant church choir assisted in the services, and the bishop standing in a Protestant pulpit read from a Protestant Bible but preached a Catholic sermon. Protestants particularly were attracted to him and found his message a revelation. It has been said, "the man I don't like is the man I don't know," and many Protestants found that to know a Catholic even a little was very different indeed from thinking they knew all about him when their only authority was secondhand and prejudiced.

So zealously did Bishop Gibbons pursue the visitation of his diocese that just as with regard to his parish of St. Bridget's it was said of him that he came to know almost every Catholic in his flock, that is, practically every member of his church in the state of North Carolina, besides a very large number of Protestants. His journal of his tour is a mine of information in great detail of the Catholics everywhere throughout the state. Within the first four weeks he had traveled nearly a thousand miles and visited sixteen towns and mission stations, confirmed a number of converts, baptized others and had come in contact with nearly five hundred widely scattered Catholics.

His zeal did not abate and for some three years there was a ceaseless round of episcopal visitation. Then came a rest from his missionary labors while from September, 1869 to October, 1870 as bishop he was in attendance at the Ecumenical Council of the Vatican. It was a rest physically but not mentally for he did not miss a single session and was an attentive listener at all the debates. As the youngest of the bishops whose youth and inexperience imposed upon him a discreet silence, his faithful attendance gave him an education in Church affairs that was precious beyond words. After thus coming in contact with all the great ecclesiastics of the Church in the capital of Christianity he came back to his poverty-stricken diocese of North Carolina—for that is the only adequate term to use of it in the conditions that had developed after the war—more zealous than ever to preach to his flock the word of God as taught by the Church.

His contact with Protestants in his missionry labors throughout North Carolina gave him as he said himself an insight into the point of view of those outside the Church that was extremely important in putting him into sympathetic relations with the American people generally. His biogra-

pher, Mr. Allen Sinclair Will, sums up the effect
of these years in North Carolina very well. "He
was not less a Catholic when he left North Carolina than he went there. In fact it seems that the
foundations of his belief had been strengthened by
opposition; but he had acquired a broad charity,
a wide horizon of view, from which he never separated himself in later life, and which stamped him
preëminently as a friend of men of other creeds."
Above all it is well said that "he conceded to well
disposed persons not of his faith a desire equal
to his own for the truths of Christianity. In all
works inspired by the brotherhood of man he maintained cordial contact and coöperation with them."
The effect produced upon Bishop Gibbons during
his work in North Carolina was of the greatest
value in forming his character as an American and
a Catholic and made him the representative Catholic American of the country when as the Archbishop of Baltimore, the representative prelate of
the United States in its oldest See he came to be
also a cardinal of the Roman Catholic Church.

It was this experience among the scattered Catholics in North Carolina while at the same time he
was brought in contact with so many Protestants,
that suggested to Bishop Gibbons the writing of
the book, *The Faith of Our Fathers*. To many

it might seem that his intensely difficult occupation in making the visitation of his diocese under circumstances that would try any man's soul, would prove so exhaustive of energy that almost the last thing in the world he would think of would be the writing of a book. Bishop Gibbons however knew that the principal reason why a great many people stayed outside of the Catholic Church, or were bigoted and intolerant with regard to her was that they knew almost nothing about her. They often thought they knew all about her but they had obtained their information from sources that were quite incapable of providing them with the truth. History as the Comte de Maistre said had been for three hundred years before his time, that is, ever since the Reformation, a conspiracy against the truth. Governments, monarchs, the nobility, which had benefited by the confiscation of religious properties at the time of the Reformation were anxious to hear anything and everything that defamed the old Church and made them comfortable in their ill-gotten possessions. There is nothing like the corrosive influence of graft to make people see things one-sidedly.

Cardinal Gibbons' book *The Faith of Our Fathers* is one of the most widely distributed publications in this country. When it was originally published it seemed to be too simple and almost obvious to have a very wide circulation, and yet the number of copies published continued to mount year after year until probably no book except the Bible has been issued in so many copies in this country as this simple presentation of the position of the Catholic Church outlined by a master hand in the writing of a subject that he had deeply at heart. The edition now runs close to two million of copies and the book still has a remarkable sale which probably indicates that in the next ten years another million will be sold.

Cardinal Gibbons wanted to attract people by the restatement of the doctrines of the old Church that had for nineteen hundred years known how to fit its modes of expression to the varying moods of mankind and, while always maintaining Christian dogmatic teaching intact, win them to an appreciation of the simple beauties but still more of the sweet reasonableness of Christianity. Cardinal Gibbons succeeded in doing this, in terms that would catch the attention of our generation because they represented sincerely their way of looking at religious ideas. Tucker, the assistant editor of the *Century Magazine* for some forty years, in the course of his articles on his editorial memories which appeared serially in the *Century* last year and since

in book form, declared that the most logical institution in the world is the Catholic Church. It is
this particularly that Cardinal Gibbons brought out
in his book *The Faith of Our Fathers* and it is that
which has made it so popular and enduring in influence.

In 1872 the diocese of Richmond was rendered
vacant by the death of Right Reverend Bishop
McGill. Bishop Gibbons was selected as the administrator of the diocese and later as the successor
of Bishop McGill. He continued to be for a time
the Vicar Apostolic also of North Carolina. The
bishopric of Richmond represented an advance in
the hierarchy but the state of Virginia had been so
overrun by the armies during the war and had
suffered so severely as a consequence that the difficulties of his new position were scarcely less than
those which he had found in his vicariate. In Virginia the dominant portion of the population was
as Protestant as in North Carolina and while many
of them were better educated, their prejudices were
no less deep and the new bishop had to be a missionary among them. Here, as in Richmond, we
find such notes in his diary as "preached and confirmed in a Methodist Church." Some of the notes
show the conditions of his diocese better than anything that might be said. For instance, clergymen's

salaries $320, servants' wages $333.50, organist's salary $300.

On the completion of the Cathedral of Baltimore, Bishop Gibbons was invited to preach the sermon at the consecration on May 25, 1876. No one could have been more appropriately chosen for that duty since he himself had been born not far from the cathedral and was now beginning to be recognized as one of the intellectual lights of the Catholic Church in America. His words on that occasion with regard to the relations of Church and State are the keynote of many expressions in his after life. They came very appropriately just as the United States was closing her first hundred years.

He said: "Need it be repeated that the Church is slandered when it is charged that she is inimical to liberty? The Church flourishes only in the beams of liberty. She has received more harm from the tyranny and oppression of kings and rulers than any other victim of their power. We pray for the prosperity of this our young country. In this, its centennial year, we rejoice that it has lived to show a sturdy life of liberty and regard for right and we raise the prayer, *'esto perpetua.'* "

For five years Bishop Gibbons continued his zealous, immensely difficult work as Bishop of Richmond and Vicar Apostolic of North Carolina. Then in May, 1877, he was appointed Coadjutor to the See of Baltimore with the right of succession. He had been in close association with Archbishop Bailey, his predecessor, and from Richmond had made many trips to Baltimore to relieve the archbishop of routine episcopal duties. Several years before the archbishop had proposed to ask that Bishop Gibbons be appointed as coadjutor but his humility led him to ask the archbishop to delay the decision in the matter. As a result the appointment as coadjutor came only just in time to be effective, for within a few months Archbishop Bailey died on October 3rd, and Bishop Gibbons succeeded him as the primate of the United States. Bishop Gibbons had continued after his appointment to Baltimore to reside in Richmond because he felt that he could thus fulfill his duties better, even though some of the authorities in Canon Law suggested that this might raise difficulties with regard to his right of succession to the See of Baltimore. Bishop Gibbons brushed aside the technicalities however and arranged matters so as best to facilitate the fulfillment of his obligations in the South and probably nothing is more indicative of his character than the situation which was thus created. It was typical of the man that his work for others should take precedence of any question of his own rights or claims.

From 1877 (October 19) Archbishop Gibbons began the career which was to bring him to be the most respected churchman in the country. The man had reached his full intellectual and moral status as the result of the hard things that he had gone through so successfully as pastor of St. Bridget's in Baltimore, Vicar Apostolic of North Carolina and Bishop of Richmond. He had been finely fitted for his great work of countrywide and even world-wide significance during the second half of life. Curiously enough his appointment as archbishop came just at the age of forty-three which exactly divides his life in two. In spite of this broader prelacy he was very much the archbishop of his own people and of Maryland. He came to know almost every foot of the soil of Maryland during his episcopal visitation of it and was particularly interested in the "lower counties" of Maryland where Catholicity was first planted in English America. He had a remarkable memory for names and faces and he came to know a very large number of Baltimoreans of all classes and he had a very wide acquaintance among all those who were deeply interested in Baltimore and its progress or in his native state of Maryland.

It was not long before his duties as archbishop brought him into national prominence and the first step in that direction was a visit to President Hayes made on behalf of the Catholic Indians. President Hayes "acknowledged the superiority of the Catholic missionaries over all others in benefiting the Indians" (Cardinal Gibbons' Journal, August 14, 1878). He met President Hayes on several subsequent occasions during his term of office and he wrote to Cardinal Simeoni, the papal secretary of state, "of the good feeling which now exists between the civil authorities and the Church in this country." On the occasion of the unfortunate shooting of President Garfield, Archbishop Gibbons sent a letter around to his clergy asking them for prayers for the wounded President and sent a copy of this letter with a special note of condolence to Mrs. Garfield. In the autumn of that same year Archbishop Gibbons issued what was probably the first official document from a prelate of the Catholic Church commending the national observance of Thanksgiving Day to his flock. At that time Thanksgiving Day was much less nationally celebrated than it is now. There was a certain flavor of Puritanism about it and the feeling existed in some minds that it had been established in New England with the idea of replacing in some way the old-fashioned festival of Christmas with the joyous festivities associated by tradition with that feast day and which were so repugnant to Puritan ideas. What Cardinal Gibbons thus initiated has since become the common custom of Catholic ecclesiastical authorities throughout the United States, and has lifted the Thanksgiving celebration on to a higher plane all over the country.

The work for which Cardinal Gibbons will be best known in the history of the Catholic Church in America is the Third Plenary Council of Baltimore. It was suggested by Pope Leo XIII that a Plenary Council should be held. At first Archbishop Gibbons did not favor the idea for he feared that it would reawaken feelings of intolerance and bigotry as previous councils or public announcements with regard to the progress of the Catholic Church in this country had done before. When the Pope urged it, however, Cardinal Gibbons took up the task of organizing it and to him more than any other is due the wonderful success of it. It was because of this success that the Pope in recognition of his achievement made him a cardinal. He was appointed the Apostolic Delegate, that is the direct representative of the Pope, to preside over the deliberations of the Council and made a most satisfying presiding officer. It is easy to understand that when debaters such as Archbishop Ireland of St. Paul, Archbishop Spalding of Peoria, Archbishop Ryan of Philadelphia, Archbishop Hennessy of Dubuque, with Bishop Keene of Richmond—later president of the Catholic University of Washington—and Bishop Gilmour of Cleveland, could not agree, it was no easy matter for the presiding officer to find common ground on ever so many questions on which all could stand.

The influence of Archbishop Gibbons was particularly noteworthy in the Council's proclamation of the harmony which the assembled prelates felt deep in their hearts existed between the Catholic Church and the American people. Two of the paragraphs of that proclamation, as they are to be found in the pastoral letter issued by the fathers of the Council at the conclusion of their sessions, express emphatically and unhesitatingly this great truth: "We think we can claim to be acquainted with the laws, institutions and spirit of the Catholic Church, and with the laws, institutions and spirit of our country; and we emphatically declare that there is no antagonism between them. A Catholic finds himself at home in the United States; for the influence of his Church has constantly been exercised in behalf of individual rights and popular liberties. And the right-minded American nowhere finds himself more at home than in the Catholic Church, for nowhere else can he breathe more freely that atmosphere of Divine truth, which alone can make him free.

"We repudiate with earnestness the assertion that we need to lay aside any of our devotedness to our Church, to be true Americans; the insinuation that we need to abate any of our love for our country's principles and institutions, to be faithful Catholics. To argue that the Catholic Church is hostile to our great Republic, because she teaches that 'there is no power but from God'; because, back of the events which led to the formation of the Republic she sees the Providence of God leading to that issue, and back of our country's laws the authority of God as their sanction—this is evidently so illogical and contradictory an accusation that we are astonished to hear it advanced by persons of ordinary intelligence. *We believe that our country's heroes were the instruments of the God of Nations in establishing this home of freedom; to both the Almighty and to His instruments in the work we look with grateful reverence; and to maintain the inheritance of freedom which they have left us, should it ever—which God forbid—be imperiled, our Catholic citizens will be found to stand forward, as one man, ready to pledge anew 'their lives, their fortunes and their sacred honor.'*"

The next great work for the Church that owes more probably to Cardinal Gibbons than to any other is the establishment of the Catholic University. During the discussions in the Council of Baltimore of 1866 the idea of the foundation of a national university for the training of priests and laymen was expressed. It was thought of rather as a hope than as an aim. The immediately active agent for the foundation of the university was Bishop Spalding of Peoria. He obtained from Rome the papal approval of a plan for organizing a university and this was taken up in 1884 by the Third Plenary Council of Baltimore and the establishment of a Catholic University was made part of the program of the hierarchy in the United States. Archbishop Gibbons became the head of the board of directors and remained its head until the end of his life, devoting himself to the interests of the university with tireless efforts and with the whole force of his prestige as a churchman and as a nationally recognized prelate. The success of the Catholic University and the magnificent results that have been secured in the training of very large numbers of American priests in the highest domain of culture has made it very clear that Archbishop Gibbons' recognition of the power for good that it would surely prove was not mistaken but on the contrary

represented one of those forecasts for good that he
was so often able to make.

With the success of the Council of Baltimore and
the foundation of the Catholic University as accomplished facts, it is not surprising that higher
ecclesiastical preferment should be planned for the
Archbishop of Baltimore. The death of Cardinal
McCloskey (October 10, 1885) who had been for
nearly ten years a member of the College of Cardinals left the United States, which had by this time
become a very important portion of the Church,
without a representative in the cardinalate. Everything pointed to Archbishop Gibbons as the logical
successor to Cardinal McCloskey and Pope Leo
XIII always particularly interested in the Church
in America did not long delay the choice. Soon
the news began to be bruited about that his appointment as cardinal had already been determined
upon at Rome and congratulations began to pour in
on him. When the news first came to himself his
first reaction was one of self-humiliation lest he
should not be worthy of the honor and a prayer
that somehow his shortcomings should be made up
from on High. The words in his Journal are interesting in this regard as exhibiting the character
of the man very clearly. "Should the report be
verified, may God give me, as He gave to his

servant David, a humble heart that I may bear the honor with becoming modesty and a profound sense of my own unworthiness; *'suscitans de terra inopem et de stercore erigens pauperem ut collocet eum cum principibus populi.'* "

It is easy to understand that with a man so well-known as Archbishop Gibbons to be advanced to the cardinalate in a town like Baltimore which had taken him to its heart and which delights in social pageantry, the occasion of conferring the cardinal's hat was made an ovation. Nearly the whole American hierarchy gathered in the city for the ceremony. It was preceded by an ecclesiastical procession such as had never been seen in America before. There were hundreds of students for the priesthood in line and other hundreds of the regular and secular clergy, members of the various religious orders, as well as the priests of the diocese. When a Catholic procession passes in Baltimore Protestants as well as Catholics on the streets are accustomed to uncover reverently and their homage to the new cardinal made this a particularly striking part of the day's celebration. As his biographer said: "The city prepared for a general fête and wrote the name of Gibbons on the roll of its most distinguished sons. Within the crowded cathedral sat many of the most distinguished men of his native

modern times. When he was nearly fourscore he said in a sermon on Civil and Religious Liberty in the Baltimore Cathedral (December 7, 1913), "The question arises, which is the best arrangement: the official union of Church and State or the mutual independence of both? I have nothing to say in regard to other countries, but our own friendly relation of Church and State without official union is best for us.

"The Church has tried official union of Church and State and she has tried friendly independence. In adhering to the first system she has often been hampered and restrained in her Divine mission by the encroachment of despotic governments. As far as our own country is concerned, I prefer our American system, where there are friendly relations and mutual coöperation, where both move in parallel lines without clash or conflict, each helping the other in the mission it has from God. . . ."

Very probably the best demonstration in the concrete of the success of the relations between Church and State in America is to be found in the mutual good will and even intimate friendship which existed between Cardinal Gibbons and the various presidents of the United States during the long years of his life as cardinal. With all of them there was an intimacy that made misunderstanding impossible. These men had the most perfect confidence in each other's absolute sincerity and good faith and shared the conviction that their one idea was the highest good of the American people as they saw it.

The relations between President Cleveland and Cardinal Gibbons were very close. Both appreciated very highly the character of the other and each of them were gifted in this regard beyond the vast majority of men. In 1887 there occurred the jubilee of the ordination to the priesthood of Pope Leo XIII. President Cleveland wrote to Cardinal Gibbons to ask whether without impropriety it would not be possible for the cardinal to convey his congratulations and felicitations to the Holy Father on this happy event. Cardinal Gibbons at once called upon President Cleveland and expressed the hope that the President would not be content with a formal communication but would send some memento of his sentiments to the pontiff. He suggested further that as the centennial of the Constitution had just been commemorated, a copy of that would be one of the most appropriate gifts. President Cleveland accepted the cardinal's suggestion as a happy one. Accordingly a copy was bound in white and red superbly printed in old English characters on vellum bearing the presentation inscrip-

tion from the President to the Pope. Pope Leo
was intensely pleased with the gift and exhibited
it in his private apartments with the presentation
page open so that visitors might see its provenance.

It was not long after this incident of the presentation of the Constitution of the United States to
Pope Leo XIII by President Cleveland, and its acceptance by the Pope as a specially acceptable gift
for his jubilee, that Senator Mark Hanna, the Ohio
politician, who knew men so well, used that famous
expression which has been so often quoted. His
influence in the election of McKinley as President
and the place that he came to occupy in the political
life of the country as a consequence, made his expression of very striking significance. When in the
last decade of the nineteenth century socialism
seemed to be threatening the peace and political
solidarity of this country, he declared that there
were two institutions which it seemed to him assured the proper control of socialistic tendencies in
this country. These were the Supreme Court of
the United States and the Roman Catholic Church.
At the time when he spoke there had been very
large immigration to this country for years and a
great many of the immigrants came from countries
where they were under strong Catholic influence and
already the Catholic Church in this country was

organizing them in congregations, and the politically wise Mark Hanna felt that the future might well be trusted to education and consequent respect for law. Hence his declaration that the Supreme Court and the Roman Catholic Church were the safeguards against political radicalism.

The most interesting intellectual trait of Cardinal Gibbons was his wonderful memory. He had an unfailing power of recollecting names and faces that very few people have and then his remembrance for facts and dates of any special significance was a never-ending source of marvel to those close to him. He had besides that rare combination in connection with these other modes of memory, a power of recalling words that was very striking. He could recite long passages of poetry or briefer paragraphs of prose that contained striking thoughts, word for word, long after he had heard them or repeated them previously. Down to the very end of his life he could write a sermon or more important discourse and read it over twice and then repeat it almost word for word, apparently without any effort and certainly without any impairment of his expression of significant values in it as would lessen its power to reach his hearers' minds and hearts. Undoubtedly this marvelous memory of his was of very great value to him and meant much for his successful achievement. Some of those who are not possessed of it affect to despise memory, or at least make little of it, on the score that it is only a conventional power of reproducing thoughts that come from others and has little to do with that faculty of independent thought which is the highest of mental traits; but it must not be forgotten that memory has the greatest possible significance in supplying material for thought and affording precedents for judgments that are of primary importance in practical life.

Cardinal Gibbons possessed at all times, though it was particularly noticeable in the maturer years of his life, a fine power of grasping the significance of complicated problems, seeing the clew through them, and reaching a conclusion so rapidly that it seemed almost like intuition. Those who knew him the best have dwelt upon this. Some of them have suggested that the cardinal seemed to have a power of perception that was almost uncanny. At times when you merely introduced a question to him and felt that it would require much more explanation, he grasped the whole subject and reached a definite conclusion with regard to it. This was not the result of any overhastiness to be rid of problems and find their solution at once, for far above the great majority of men he was prudent and rashness is one of the faults that has never even been hinted at his regard. We have used the word intuition, and undoubtedly there is some such faculty in many people which enables them to see through the meaning of things without the need of that slower reasoning which others require. It has often been said that intuition is a feminine quality and that it is noted best in action particularly where a woman's love guides her rather than her mind alone. After all we have come to realize in recent years that there is a very definite significance for the use of the word heart as meaning something deeper in human thinking than merely the mind.

The heart as "the sum total of kindly impulses" often enables those whose hearts are touched to see through a mass of details or a maze of difficulties ever so much better than understanding alone would help them to do. In this way a woman's intuition where the interests of those whom she loves deeply, husband, son, brother, are concerned, is often the most precious guide in the world. There are a certain number of men, usually those who have talent of such high order as to amount almost to genius, who have this feminine quality. It is mainly noticeable in matters where the deepest interests of humanity are concerned. Cardinal Gibbons had often come to him for decision the great problems relating to Church and humanity and it was with regard to these that his friends noted his power of intuition. It is not surprising that he should have had it under the circumstances though it is another index of the superior nature of the man and the wellsprings of intellectual vitality that he had within himself. It is the judgment of such men particularly that counts with regard to the great problems of humanity that lie around us in the insoluble mysteries of our relation to the universe and it is his place as a factor for the solution of these that made Cardinal Gibbons one of the powerful influences of his time in this country.

Though his biographers generally have not dwelt much on it, Cardinal Gibbons had a deep sense of humor that helped him very much on his way through life. Like his Irish ancestors he could see the humorous side even of serious things and this prevented him from letting the troubles of life weigh heavily on him. What would his forbears have been where the melancholy Atlantic beats round their island and so many internal troubles were at work without this saving trait. A typical example of the quality of Cardinal Gibbons' humor is quoted by Mr. Jacob A. Riis, in his autobiography, *The Making of an American*. "On one occasion when the Cardinal wished to excuse himself on the plea of being very tired, he explained that he had had a very wearisome day, and added: 'And I am an old man, on the sunny side of sixty.' 'On the shady side, you mean,' corrected a clergyman, who stood nearby. The old Cardinal shook his head: 'No, the sunny side—nearer Heaven.' "

Many problems demanding the enunciation of Church principles in their relation to the practical world around, came up during the course of Cardinal Gibbons' life. Probably the most interesting of these and one of the most important for the estimation of the Church in the minds of the great mass of the working people of the country was what was known as the Knights of Labor problem in America in the last decade of the nineteenth century. The Knights of Labor represented an organization of workmen throughout the country which had grown very rapidly in the eighties of the nineteenth century. Its head, Mr. Terence V. Powderly, who bore the modest title of "General Master Workman," declared before a committee of Congress in 1886 that it had a membership of 500,000, although he added "we have been credited with 5,000,000." The organization made itself felt in politics; the contract labor law forbidding the bringing of workmen into the country under contract, the Chinese exclusion act, even the Interstate Commerce Act, were all due to the political influence of this organization. President Cleveland's administration committed itself to the estabment of the Department of Labor at Washington largely because of pressure brought to bear through them.

All these were good effects but unfortunately Henry George's economic theories were securing many adherents at this time and certain socialistic and communistic as well as anarchistic theories were spreading among the laboring classes. The anarchist riot in Chicago which cost precious lives had shocked many people. It seemed as though a whole series of factors were working for the disturbance of political peace in this country. Class feelings were deeply aroused. So-called captains of industry were at work combining great industrial concerns and unfortunately lent themselves to influencing legislation unduly and above all set themselves to securing the control of politicians. It looked for a time as though there were seething elements at work within the body politic that might cause very serious trouble. Socialism seemed threatening beyond anything like its real significance and as a result feelings of suspicion were aroused against organizations of workmen.

Employers of labor, it is said, made it a point

to send agents to take note of proceedings among
the Knights of Labor at their meetings and sometimes used information thus obtained to prevent
the rise to important positions in industry of any
of those closely allied with the organization and
sometimes deprived them of their occupations. The
result was the investment of the meetings of the
Knights with sufficient secrecy to protect their proceedings from being divulged to those who might
make wrong use of them. The Church has always
been suspicious of secret societies and when the
Knights of Labor were accused before the Catholic
hierarchy of Canada as a secret society working
against religion, they were condemned as coming
under the ban of forbidden organizations and this
condemnation was sustained by the Congregation
of the Holy Office at Rome.

This action called for consideration by the hierarchy of the United States. Under the decrees of
the Third Plenary Council of Baltimore the Knights
could be condemned in the United States by the
unanimous action of the archbishops; or in case the
archbishops disagreed the case would be referred
to Rome. As the only cardinal in the United States,
Cardinal Gibbons had a very serious responsibility
placed on his shoulders in this matter. He did not
fear socialistic tendencies among the laboring

classes, as did many others, and he felt that the American Church must not be hasty in condemnation of efforts that were manifestly intended to better the condition of the working classes.

He took counsel with his friend, President Cleveland, and opened an active correspondence with Cardinal Manning in England, who has been spoken of as "the Church's apostle of labor" in the English-speaking world. But of these men encouraged him in the idea that much could be accomplished in advancing the position of the laboring classes by encouraging proper union among them. He invited Mr. Terence Powderly to Baltimore so as to have an explanation of what was exactly the purpose and extent of secrecy among the Knights of Labor. As the result of the knowledge thus secured, Cardinal Gibbons was able to place before the archbishops of the country the real status of the Knights of Labor so that in the end only two of the twelve archbishops voted for condemnation.

Cardinal Gibbons undertook next a task that his friends felt sure would end in failure. The Congregation of the Holy Office is the institution known in history as "the Inquisition." It had never reversed itself in its long history, it was said, and to suggest a favorable modification of the condemnation of the Knights of Labor seemed a hopeless

proposal. Cardinal Gibbons felt that to condemn
the order was to condemn labor and that condemnation might force the Knights into socialistic tendencies. He felt that what he termed "the simple rights
of humanity and justice" were being denied. When
the cardinal went over for the reception of the red
hat, he was resolved to place the problem of the
Knights of Labor before the authorities in Rome
at this time. He knew that there was very great
opposition. He knew that a great many churchmen in other countries were afraid of socialistic
tendencies. He wrote a memorable epistle which
was really a brief for the Knights of Labor to
Cardinal Simeoni, Prefect of the Congregation of
Propaganda, which was then in charge of the
Church in the United States since this country was
as yet considered a missionary country. He provided an opening for a new judgment on the part
of the Holy Office with regard to the affairs of the
Knights of Labor in the United States by pointing out how different were religious conditions in
the United States and Canada. This was particularly true as regards Lower Canada where the
people were almost entirely Catholic.

This letter has sometimes been called "the Christian charter of labor" in this country. Gradually
the efforts of Cardinal Gibbons and of Cardinal

Manning made themselves felt and others began
to see that radical action of the Church in the matter would surely be a mistake of policy at least and
that principles were not involved in anything like
the way that was supposed. The result was a vic-
tory for the Knights of Labor and for the archbishops of the United States, but above all, for
Cardinal Gibbons which brought him prominently
before the world. He made the Church's position
with regard to labor very clear. This did not come
about without misunderstanding on the part of
many of the conservatives and Cardinal Gibbons
was even caricatured by *Puck,* the American comic
journal, as blessing the mob in its work of destruc-
tion, but his deeply humanitarian feelings came to
make themselves felt very generally and the result
was a new background for judgment as to labor's
rights and privileges.

Only a few years later Pope Leo XIII (1891)
issued his great encyclical, *Rerum novarum,* usually
known in English as "The Condition of Labor," in
which he laid down the principles upon which the
workman must be dealt with. The great pontiff
did not hesitate to say that "some remedy must be
found quickly for the misery and wretchedness
which weigh so heavily and unjustly at this moment
on the majority of the working classes." He even

7777

ventured to say very emphatically that unfortunately "the working men had been surrendered all isolated and helpless to the hard heartedness of employers," so that "a small number of very rich men had been able to lay upon the teeming masses of the laboring poor a yoke little better than slavery itself." That encyclical, though issued thirty-five years ago, is still a gospel of the rights of labor.

Other problems relating to important Church matters came up for decision before the American hierarchy in which Cardinal Gibbons' influence was felt always for thoroughgoing conservatism and yet for that progressiveness which must be associated with the Church here in America. Above all, the school problem had to be worked out and as we know ever so much better now, on the question of religious teaching in the schools depends the growth and maintenance of the Church in numbers. Under Archbishop Ireland's direction certain experiments had been made in the schools at Faribault and Stillwater in Minnesota, by which it was hoped to secure such coöperation between Catholics and the public schools as would provide a *modus vivendi* that would prove economic and efficient for both parties. The parochial school buildings in Faribault and Stillwater were leased to the district school commissioners during the school hours only.

The sisters taught during these hours and gave no religious instruction during school time. After school hours catechism was taught and at eight-thirty in the morning before the regular school hour the children attended Mass. At all other hours and on Sunday the school buildings were at the exclusive disposition of the parish.

These experiments gave rise to widespread discussion. The danger which many of the Catholic bishops and priests feared was that after a time the civic authorities would assert their influence in other ways over the scholastic curriculum and the real purpose of the Catholic school be lost. On the other hand a great many non-Catholics feared that this might be an entering wedge for the introduction of sectarian influences into the public-school system. It is a little difficult to understand now how bitter the controversy grew. Cardinal Gibbons was the conciliator in the matter and his influence with the Holy See drew from Pope Leo XIII a letter to the Cardinal of Baltimore in which the Pope set forth that the decisions of the Council of Baltimore in the school questions were to be faithfully observed and every endeavor must be made to multiply the Catholic schools and to raise their standards and equipment; but the public schools were not to be condemned since cases might occur in which it was permissible to attend them. Cardinal Satolli who was then the papal delegate to the United States laid down certain principles which emphasized the necessity for the religious training of youth but left to local conditions and the bishop of each diocese a certain liberty in working out the plan by which this should be accomplished.

The school question was scarcely settled when another and more important subject for debate came up in what was known as Cahenslyism. Peter Cahensly was only the secretary of a Catholic society for the protection of German immigrants. Its first purpose was that of promoting the spiritual welfare of settlers in foreign countries but it assumed the duty of preserving the nationality and language of those who emigrated from Europe. In a certain way the problem thus raised affected other countries and other nationalities besides the German. There was an alliance among the foreign societies in this country to secure a certain independence of their own within the Church and obtain the appointment of bishops of their own nationality. They pointed out that there probably had been immense losses to the Church by the lapsing of immigrants from their religion and that this loss amounted to between fifteen and twenty

millions in the American republic. These statistics
have been seriously doubted and above all Bishop
Canevin of Pittsburgh a few years ago showed
how insubstantial they were. The whole question
aroused deep attention and the Cahensly element
brought it to the attention of the Pope.

Cardinal Gibbons was intent that the Church
in this country should continue homogeneous, like
the nation. He feared the disintegrating effects
of the different nationalities maintaining their own
languages, their home customs, their foreign language newspapers, all emphasized by their own prelates. What happened during the World War has
illuminated very strikingly Cardinal Gibbons' expressions and feelings in that matter. As a matter
of fact, while great influence was brought to bear
by European countries in the matter, the German
Catholics of this country, as a mass, were not behind
the Cahensly movement. As with regard to the
school question, it is a little difficult for us now,
though not a full generation away, to understand
how bitter were the animosities that were aroused
and how fraught with danger for the peace of the
country was the movement. Fortunately Cardinal
Gibbons' large-hearted patriotism and the esteem
in which he was held by all had very much to do
with gradually clearing the air here in America

and making the situation manifest in its true significance to the authorities in Rome.   Hyphenated
Americanism is now a thing of the past, made so by
the Great War, but Cardinal Gibbons' foresight was
extremely important in eliminating from American
life what might have proved very discordant elements had they been allowed to grow as luxuriantly
as they threatened to do at the height of the Cahensly movement.   We were a much more united
people in 1917 when we entered the War as the
result of Cardinal Gibbons' prudence.

Very probably the most important work accomplished by Cardinal Gibbons in his official position
and as an American citizen was that which concerned our newly acquired possessions after the
Spanish-American War.   The Philippines particularly had been very largely under the influence of
the Church and the friars had acquired a position
even in the political government to such an extent
that their replacement threatened to bring about
collapse of authority.   President Taft, talking at
the Catholic Summer School of America, declared
that there was no higher tribute that could be paid
to the Catholic Church and the beneficence of its influence than the fact that an absolutely uncivilized
people in the Philippines had been raised by its
missionaries to a level of civilization where on the

transfer to the United States they were almost ready for independent government. During the course of this process the missionaries, that is, the friars or members of religious orders had quite naturally come to assume many of the functions of government. Spanish officials were few and frequently changed and the friars resided permanently in the country and the people came to look to them as their representatives in authority. Religious orders constituted the first schools of agriculture in Europe. It is not surprising then that in the Philippines they raised the value of their land by their skill and attention. As they had no heirs except their brethren their possessions accumulated and were added to by gifts and bequests from pious Church members.

The question of these valuable friars' lands then became one of the most important for the settlement of Philippine political disaffection. Negotiations in the matter were difficult and in spite of the willingness of the United States government to do all that it could, it was hampered by the political difficulties inevitably involved here in America if United States authorities should even seem to be generous to the friars. Negotiations had come to a standstill when Cardinal Gibbons was consulted by President Roosevelt and offered to find a way to settlement. President Roosevelt sent Secretary Taft who had been the Civil Governor of the Philippines to Baltimore to consult Cardinal Gibbons before going to Rome for a complete settlement. It was through the cardinal's influence that the whole question was taken up at Rome and expedited to a successful and satisfactory conclusion. There then remained the problems connected with the reorganization of the hierarchy in the Philippines, Porto Rico and Cuba, and for this Cardinal Gibbons visited Rome and after a series of consultations with Pope Leo XIII and the members of the Roman Curia the idea of sending American bishops to the Islands thoroughly in touch with the American system of relations between Church and State was worked out to the great benefit of all concerned.

There remained certain more or less inevitable developments in the Church situation in these newly acquired American possessions which had to be worked out carefully. Whenever there was friction in the Philippines or in the West Indies, Cardinal Gibbons was appealed to and his close touch with President Roosevelt brought about a satisfactory solution of the problems. Between President Roosevelt and after him President Taft and Cardinal Gibbons there was always the friendliest understanding and the recognition that they were all intent on the benefit of all concerned and especially the application of American principles to these portions of the union. When legislation against the Church or at least that would greatly hamper its ministrations threatened once in Cuba, Cardinal Gibbons conferred with President Taft and Mr. Knox, Secretary of State, who proved most sympathetic. President Taft said that he was sending a fleet to the Argentine Republic to participate in its centenary, bearing General Leonard Wood whom the President would instruct to stop at Havana with the fleet and have a conversation with President Gomez on the subject of the proposed adverse laws. President Gomez expressed his conviction that the laws would not be passed and that if passed they would certainly be vetoed. The papal Secretary of State thanked Cardinal Gibbons for his intervention in the matter.

When it became clear that Pope Leo XIII after his long years as pope was approaching the end of life, Cardinal Gibbons sailed for Europe so as to take part in the conclave for the election of a new pope. This was the first time that an American cardinal had ever taken part in the election. Owing to the exercise of the veto power which by custom had become vested in the Austrian government, Cardinal Rampolla who like so many others according to the old phrase entered the conclave pope but came out cardinal, failed of election. The College of Cardinals then chose Cardinal Sarto of Venice as the successor of Leo XIII. Cardinal Sarto however who had no inkling of the possibility of his being chosen and had actually bought a return ticket to Venice when he set out for Rome, was overcome at the prospect of the burden thus to be placed on his shoulders and refused to accept it. It has been said very probably with truth that when the representations of Italian cardinal friends failed to move the Patriarch of Venice, a message from Cardinal Gibbons sent to him through Cardinal Satolli turned the scale in favor of his acceptance. The force of the idea that the cardinal representative of the western Catholic world, where the Church was so progressive, added the weight of his advice also to others, swayed Cardinal Sarto's mind and he became that "pope of the people, the children and the Eucharist" who meant so much for the revival of the spirit of piety in the Church at the beginning of the twentieth century.

In October, 1911, occurred the celebration of the jubilee of Cardinal Gibbons as a priest, that is the fiftieth year of his ordination. The occasion became a national event. Archbishop Glennon of St. Louis made the address for the ecclesiastical celebration of that event. In doing so he probably summed up Cardinal Gibbons' place in modern history better than any other could hope to do, for his position and his long years of association with the Cardinal of Baltimore gave him opportunity to know him and appreciate his services to humanity and to his country better than any one else. Archbishop Glennon said, "In the defense of social order; in the promotion of human right; in the supreme effort to maintain the social fabric and the institutions of our beloved country, no voice in all the broad land is to-day as potent, no personality so influential as that of our beloved Cardinal.

"Indeed the position of Cardinal Gibbons is unique not alone in Church history, but in world history as well. There have been great Cardinals in the centuries that are gone—Wolsey, Richelieu—but the opportunity of their greatness arose in part at least from the union of Church and State that then existed, and history tells us that they served their king with far more zeal than they served their God. We have had great Cardinals in modern times— Wiseman, Manning, Newman—and again in part their greatness came from the noble defense they made of a Church that was persecuted.

"We may not deny their greatness, their learning, their consecration; but, unlike any one member of either group, our Cardinal stands with the same devotion to his country as Richelieu had for France, cultivating a citizenship as unstained as Newman, and while reaching out to a broader democracy than even Cardinal Manning, he still remains preëminent in his unquestioned devotion to Holy Church.

"And so, my friends, you have before you some of the titles his Eminence has to our respect and reverence; so many reasons why you should thank God that he so blest His servant and thereby blest us all.

"Priest, Bishop, Cardinal, philosopher, lawgiver, chancellor, yes, and let us not omit through all these high sounding titles that other—the first we notice, the last we may forget—

> " 'For he is gracious if he be observed
>   He hath a tear for pity and a hand
>   Open as day for meeting charity.'

"Yes, Cardinal Gibbons is a kindly, gentle man." Very probably one of the most touching things in the life of Cardinal Gibbons is the scene which has been described by his biographer evidently from Cardinal Gibbons' own relation of it, of his parting with Archbishop Ryan of Philadelphia. The two great churchmen, whose years rang along very nearly parallel, had become closer and closer as the years rolled on. They had been intimate companions as well as faithful colleagues in all important Church matters during half a century. Gradually they had seen their contemporaries disappear from the scene one after the other and they were almost alone when manifestly Archbishop Ryan's term of life was approaching. That last parting might possibly be thought of as entirely preoccupied with thoughts of another world. As a matter of fact what the two great churchmen talked about was their country and the hope of its future greatness and their confidence that the Catholic Church by keeping it conservative would lead to the enhancement of that greatness.

As the story is told, "A few days before Ryan's death, the Cardinal went to Philadelphia to visit him. Entering the sick room, he placed his hand upon the Archbishop's brow and said softly:

" 'Your Grace does not know me.'

"The Archbishop, who had been hovering on the verge of unconsciousness, answered in a sudden rally of his faculties:

" 'I know every tone of your Eminence's voice and now, as ever, I am convinced that you are the instrument of Providence for every good thing for our Church and country.'

"The sick prelate, seemingly endowed with new strength, talked for some minutes with the Cardinal. They spoke of men and things long gone, of mutual hopes that had blossomed or withered. Naturally their thoughts turned to the future of the nation, which they had served so faithfully.

" 'If we keep America conservative,' said the Archbishop, 'no country will be as great as this.' "

When the United States entered the World War, Cardinal Gibbons at once expressed his complete readiness to support his country in any and every way and declared that "there must be no shirkers." On his eighty-second birthday the year before, he had expressed his approval of the training camps and their value "to safeguard the nation, build up its manhood and fuse its foreign strains." Above all he thought them valuable because they brought "the rich man and the poor man together on an equal footing and taught them that they owe an equal allegiance." The week after the declaration of war the archbishops of the United States met and on the proposal of Cardinal Gibbons adopted a set of resolutions which appealed deeply to the patriotic sense of the country. Cardinal Gibbons sent the resolutions the next day to President Wilson, who called them "very remarkable resolutions" and declared that they warmed his heart and "made me proud indeed that men of such large influence should act in so large a sense of patriotism and so admirable a spirit of devotion to our common country."

The opening paragraphs of the resolutions were as follows:

"Standing firmly upon our solid Catholic tradition and history, from the very foundation of this nation, we affirm in this hour of stress and trial our most sacred and sincere loyalty and patriotism toward our country, our government and our flag.

"Moved to the very depths of our hearts by the stirring appeal of the President of the United States, and by the action of our National Congress, we accept whole-heartedly and unreservedly the decree of that legislative authority proclaiming this country to be in a state of war.

"We have prayed that we might be spared the dire necessity of entering the conflict, but now that war has been declared we bow in obedience to the summons to bear our part in it with fidelity, with courage and with the spirit of sacrifice which as loyal citizens we are bound to manifest for the defense of the most sacred rights, and the welfare of the whole nation."

Cardinal Gibbons' love for his country was deep and cordial and it was constantly bubbling up for expression. In his *Retrospect of Fifty Years* he said, "My countrymen and my fellow Catholics will forgive me if I seem to yearn over this Church and this people; but I do so because I believe both the

American Church and the American people to be precious in the sight of God and designed, each one in its proper sphere, for a glorious future." As Rev. Father Felix has suggested, these are an echo of his words in Rome years before when he was created cardinal in 1887: "I belong to the country where the civil government holds over us the ægis of its protection without interfering with us in the legitimate exercise of our mission as ministers of the Gospel of Christ. Our country has liberty without license and authority without despotism. The men who would endeavor to undermine the laws and institutions of this country deserve the fate of those who laid profane hands on the Ark."

The official biographer of Cardinal Gibbons, Mr. Allen Sinclair Will, in concluding his monumental life of our great cardinal, one of the important American biographies of our day, summed up very succinctly and yet very truthfully, the character and the reasons for the influence Cardinal Gibbons exerted over his generation. He emphasized particularly Cardinal Gibbons' personal habits of devotion and prayer "as the first and chief duty of every day" and as the source and inspiration of all the "simple acts of kindness to all without partition of creed or race" which made his life such a striking one for all those who knew him even a little inti-

mately. That life was a great apologia for religion
and what religion can accomplish in making a man
a better citizen, a fonder lover of his kind, and
an unselfish representative of all that is best in
human nature.

His biographer said of him: "With him religion
was a real thing—the greatest reality of life—and
his eyes were fixed on it as his support and his guide
in manifold labors that left an indelible stamp upon
the fabric of contemporaneous history.

"That he was a Christian was a glory of all
Christians; that he was a Catholic was a glory of all
Catholics.

"To those who saw him from afar, his wider acts
of accomplishment were the measure of him; but
what impression remained with the hundreds, even
thousands, who felt directly in the course of his
long life the personal force of the man, who heard
his voice, touched his hand, came under the power
of his striking and distinctive personality? Catholic
and Protestant, Jew and Gentile, Pope and President, statesman and street urchin, the high and the
low of many degrees, would frame their answers
differently; but all who knew him shared in one com-
posite thought, overshadowing and embracing other
thoughts of him, the blend of his legacy to his fellow-
men—Here was a man of God."

So far as he was a man above men—though the cardinal himself would have been the first to deprecate any such tribute, he would have said very candidly that he owed whatever there was in his life worth while to two things—his adhesion to the Catholic Church and his personal habit of prayer which he felt enabled him to be the channel for divine influences for himself and others.

Cardinal Gibbons' own faith and adhesion to the Catholic Church was so intense as to leave no room in his mind for doubts. Difficulties there might be, but as Cardinal Newman said, a thousand difficulties cannot make a single doubt. Father Felix Ward, the Passionist, who was a close personal friend of the cardinal's, tells how once on a walk with his Eminence he quoted the words of Cardinal Newman. "Either the Catholic Religion is verily the coming of the unseen world into this, or there is nothing positive, nothing dogmatic, nothing real in any of our notions as to whence we come or whither we go." The cardinal added: "There would be nothing for us but black despair, if the Church is not divine."

A few years ago when Cardinal Vaughan of England died and his life was published, one of the surprises that struck most people was his habit of prayer. Here was a man who was extremely busy, concerned with many important affairs, with scarcely enough time in the twenty-four hours to do all that he wanted to do, and yet he actually spent hours every day in prayer. He himself declared that so far from interfering with his work prayer made it possible for him to do as much as he did and that without it he should have been lost and could not hope to accomplish so much. He would have lacked confidence in his own powers and in his own motives and he would have worked with less enthusiasm and less devotion, but above all he felt that surely he would have missed potent direction that meant so much for him and that enabled him to go on.

Cardinal Gibbons was such another man. He was an early riser. Of course he said his Mass every morning but he spent an hour before Mass in meditating on the life of the Lord and Master, taking some passage of the New Testament as a text for his thoughts. "Only in meditation the Mystery speaks to us." He said to his confessor once, "With ever increasing demands on me I could never say I have not time to pray." He never missed his visit to the Blessed Sacrament in the evening. "A visit to our Lord in the Blessed Sacrament," he said, "dissipates the worldly mist that may have enveloped you and brings you nearer to the God of light and diffuses around you a spirit of heavenly tranquillity."

He often said that he thought he owed his power to sleep even when many problems were clamoring for solution to his habit of prayer and the fact that he could say whole-heartedly "Thy Will be done."

The rosary was very precious to him. He said it daily and made it a point whenever social obligations took him out in the evening to say it on the way. Those who went with him in his carriage shared the rosary with him and he felt that it did them all good. His household became inevitably a focus of prayer and it is interesting and extremely significant to realize that out of that household, that is from among the members of the circle who for a longer or shorter time shared the home life of the cardinal, there came more bishops for the United States than from any other similar environment. So true was this that the cardinal's home was spoken of as a "nursery of bishops."

Some of the tributes that were paid to the cardinal after his death give an excellent idea of the esteem in which he was held by our most distinguished men in this country because of his wisdom and his patriotism. Ex-President Taft for instance said of him, "The Cardinal was a man of most kindly heart and broad vision, of statesmanlike views on great questions and with indomitable courage in expressing them. He represented the highest moral aspirations of the community and all classes of good people, without regard to creed, were grateful to him for his constant effort to lift its members out of sordid ambitions and pursuits and to aim at higher things. As a non-Catholic I am glad to bear witness to the power for good which Cardinal Gibbons exercised. He was an able churchman and patriotic citizen." On hearing of the death of the cardinal, President Harding dispatched the following message to the auxiliary bishop of Baltimore: "In common with all our people, I mourn the death of Cardinal Gibbons. His long and notable service to the country and to the Church makes us all his debtors. He was ever ready to lend his encouragement to any movement for the betterment of his fellowmen. He was the very finest type of citizen and churchman. It was my good fortune to know him personally and I held him in highest esteem and veneration. His death is a distinct loss to the country, but it brings to fuller appreciation a great and admirable life."

JOHN, CARDINAL FARLEY *

THIRD AMERICAN CARDINAL

ON the occasion of the elevation of Archbishop Farley of New York to membership in the College of Cardinals, Cardinal Gibbons of Baltimore was invited to deliver the address. The keynote of that address was contained in the words, "It is not the cardinal that ennobles a man; it is the man that ennobles the cardinal." That is surely the best formula with which to begin the life of Cardinal Farley for to those who knew him he was a man of very noble and precious character who though of comparatively short stature stood head and shoulders above other men because of his moral worth as a man. His one purpose in life was to be just as good a churchman as possible. No one knew better than he however that though he was only a naturalized citizen of the United States and not a native that his

---

* The sketch of Cardinal Farley by Right Reverend Michael J. Lavelle (New York Paulist Press, 1919) forms the basis of this article. As Monsignor Lavelle was for some forty years very close to Cardinal Farley while he was going through the steps of ecclesiastical preferment as a priest, auxiliary bishop, archbishop and cardinal, the material that he has gathered is authentic and authoritative.

CARDINAL FARLEY

duties as a churchman were not fulfilled as they
should be unless he were at the same time a worthy
citizen of this country deeply intent•on furthering its
interests in every possible way that he could. Coming from Ireland he knew the precious heritage of
liberty that was in the United States and his constant thought was to help the citizens in the country
to preserve that liberty so that it might go down
as an unfailing deposit to future generations.

John Murphy Farley was born at Newtown
Hamilton, County Armagh, Ireland, April, 1842.
His family were plain farming people in reasonably
comfortable circumstances, able to afford their children a good education. One of his brothers, Ed-
ward Farley, emigrated to New York and became
a rather prominent merchant in the city. His ma-
ternal uncle, Patrick Murphy, was for years a member of the well-known firm of Solomon & Son. The
future cardinal's preliminary studies were made near
his native home, but Irish schoolmasters have ever
been known for their thoroughness, and he secured
an excellent grasp of Latin and Greek and of funda-
mentals in mathematics.

He came to this country in 1864 and immediately
entered St. John's College, Fordham, which has
now become Fordham University. At that time
St. John's was a flourishing institution. It had been

founded originally by Archbishop Hughes about twenty-five years before, and he had transferred it to the Jesuits from St. Mary's in Kentucky in 1846. This fact brought a number of southern students to the college and the war had prevented their further attendance, but the college had continued to progress and was looked upon at that time as very probably one of the most important of the Catholic colleges in the country.

At Fordham young Farley displayed brilliant talents and a capacity for learning which attracted attention and led many people to feel that here was a young man who would surely make more than an ordinary success of life. He was particularly expert in mathematics and in languages. He had moreover a deep interest in English literature cultivated for its own sake because there was not very much encouragement for purely English studies at that time. Education was looked upon as formation of mind rather than information of memory and mental discipline rather than interest was the fundamental note in the arrangement of studies. Young Farley was however very much interested in the cultivation of various modes of expression in English. He developed a facility and elegance in writing verse which according to those who knew him at the time might with appropriate cultivation have enabled him to attain a power of poetic expression that would have brought with it very definite prestige.

At the end of a year at Fordham he entered upon his theological studies in the provincial seminary of New York which was then situated at Troy. Here he distinguished himself so remarkably in his studies that at the end of a single year he was chosen by Archbishop McCloskey on the recommendation of the rector of the seminary to continue and finish his studies in theology and the subjects related to it at the North American College in Rome usually spoken of simply as the American College.

Almost needless to say this experience of three years at the American College was extremely valuable to a man of Farley's character for he had a broad foundation of education in the classics and deep interests in classical Rome. He had developed various historical interests besides and indeed was known for his attraction to this form of study. Between the remains of classical Rome and the memorials of the Church of the Fathers and of the Middle Ages and the Renaissance, the young American College student obtained a magnificent background on which to appreciate the significance of historical information. He was present at the canonization of the Japanese martyrs in 1867 and that completed the background of Church history for him since it added a touch of interest in the history of the missions, recalled all of Francis Xavier's great work and that of his successors in the East, and above all brought back to attention the fact that some of the Japanese deprived of priests had yet succeeded in certain parts of Japan in keeping alive the knowledge and the spirit of Christianity and had been ready to welcome the Catholic missionaries when, centuries later, they came once more into the celestial kingdom. For a young man's mind nothing could be more broadening than the focusing of all these interests during the very impressionable years under twenty-five.

One of the fruits of Cardinal Farley's years in Rome was a great devotion to St. Philip Neri who is often spoken of as the Apostle of Rome. St. Philip who is the founder of the Oratory, that is of the religious congregation, the Oratorians, a body of priests who devote themselves to missionary work among the educated youth of cities, was a most lovable character. From a number of conversations that I had with the cardinal while trying to sketch the background of St. Philip's life for my volume *The Century of Columbus*, it was very evident that he had tried above all to model his life

after that of St. Philip. It was among the Oratorians founded by St. Philip that Newman and
Faber and many of the distinguished converts of
the Oxford or Tractarian movement in England
found their vocations and their opportunities for
work. Cardinal Farley's favorite spiritual reading
was the life of St. Philip. He gave me a copy of
Capecelatro's life of St. Philip and while reading
that I came to realize that it represented one of
the best keys to the cardinal's own life.

There was another distinct advantage in young
Farley's stay in Rome in that he was present in
the capital of Christendom during the whole period
of the Vatican Council. This enabled him to know
by sight at least the great prelates of the Church,
to get in touch with their personalities and have
it brought home to him what each of them had accomplished in his diocesan work, but also in the intellectual order for the benefit of the Church. It
is this touch with mature minds who have done
great good work that is the best possible incentive
to the young mind to pursue its own studies seriously quite apart from any necessity there may be
of study because of various academic obligations.
All during his life as archbishop and cardinal, Cardinal Farley referred to the precious privilege that
had thus been his of seeing the prelates of the

Church assembled from all quarters, attending their deliberations at certain times, meeting many of them and realizing what a scholarly yet simple-minded body of men they were. He was ordained June 11, 1870, by Cardinal Patrizi and some six weeks later left the Eternal City for New York where his duties in the ministry were to be carried on.

Already there were rumblings of the Italian revolution and as the declaration of war between France and Germany had been made on July 19, 1870, it was evident that there might not be possibility of further intervention on the part of the French emperor for the maintenance of papal authority. Father Farley's departure at the beginning of August came just before the Italian invasion of Rome and he was spared the pain of witnessing that sad event and the retirement of the Pope within the Vatican from which up to the present time he has not issued. Father Farley's years in Rome had been under the old-time papal dispensation with all the glory of religious processions in the streets and the demonstration of tender feelings of the people for their pontiff, but all that was now at an end. To have seen that phase of history however was to have acquired a special background for the understanding of Italian history as well as the history of the Church that could not have been secured in any other way. Those who later on in life were sometimes surprised at the breadth and depth of Cardinal Farley's knowledge of men and things and of political affairs in Europe, forgot that he had been in intimate touch with events in history which enabled him to understand a great many affairs of importance better than could ever be hoped for from the merely academic student of historical events.

Father Farley's first assignment after his return to America was as assistant to the pastor at New Brighton, Staten Island. This was a full quarter century and more before the time when Staten Island came to be included within the boundaries of greater New York and New Brighton was a country parish comparatively little disturbed by its propinquity to the metropolis of New York from which it was separated by the width of the Bay with extremely inadequate ferry service. Here he was drawn into what was quite literally country parish work and he gave himself to it whole-heartedly. He became deeply interested in the parishioners and all the phases of parish activities and demonstrated rather strikingly that personal characteristic of devotion to the task in hand which was to be so marked in later life. Whatever was the duty assigned was

God's work and therefore deserved every atom of attention and devotion no matter how comparatively trivial from a material standpoint it might seem to be. His stay in Brighton altogether was less than two years, but the older people of the little town continued to remember him very cordially until the last day of his life and followed his rise in the ecclesiastical world with hearty attention and good wishes.

In 1872 with the promotion to the bishopric of Albany, of Rev. Francis McNierney who had been secretary to Archbishop McCloskey, Father Farley was appointed to the secretaryship. This constituted his first step on the rungs of the ladder of ecclesiastical promotion. His years in Rome, his wide acquaintance with the authorities of the Eternal City, his deep interest and love for the liturgy of the Church, and his proficiency in Canon Law for which his Roman studies had given him a special liking and afforded a magnificent foundation, all fitted him eminently for this position. Besides he was a man of extremely methodical habits and this is needed as a characteristic of the secretary to an archbishop. It was not long before it came to be recognized that there was another quality of his which had not been noted before and which made his appointment very fitting. This was his felicity in correspondence. It is a very valuable trait to be able to say "no" without hurting feelings. Almost needless to say the secretary of an archbishop has on many occasions to say "no" for permissions and indults are asked that cannot be granted and yet it is gracious to be able to refuse without hurting the feelings of the applicant who means well enough as a rule but has to be told that what he asks is impossible or at least inadvisable under the circumstances.

Father Farley soon attracted the cordial attention of the clergy and the people in this position which necessarily makes him the connecting link between the archbishop and his flock as well as his priests. One who knew him very well did not hesitate to say that "he won the hearts of the clergy and the people by his affability, sympathy and resource." For more than a dozen years Father Farley continued to occupy this position always exhibiting the same lovable traits of character. The elevation of his prelate Archbishop McCloskey to the cardinalate in 1875 reflected something of prestige on the position of his secretary and his visit to Rome with the cardinal in 1878 when Pope Leo was elected to the papacy added to that prestige. It was not surprising that after these dozen of years in the position he was nominated as papal chamberlain in January,

1884 though it is more than a little surprising that that appointment was delayed quite so long as it was. It is understood now that the delay was due more to Father Farley's own modesty and his unwillingness to be distinguished above other priests of the diocese, some of whom had spent long years in hard work in the ministry without any further ecclesiastical preferment than their pastorates. It was he himself a little later who was to introduce the custom of providing through the Roman authorities dignities in larger number for his loyal clergy.

In August, 1884, Monsignor Farley was appointed to the pastorate of St. Gabriel's Church in East 37th Street. This was a very populous parish composed mostly of working people very closely attached to the Church and ready to take advantage of all the spiritual opportunities afforded them. He succeeded in winning the hearts of his parishioners and during the eighteen years of his pastorate the very closest of kindly relations existed between pastor and flock. Monsignor Farley was deeply interested particularly in the development of the parochial school in connection with the parish. He wanted to make it just as far as possible the equal of the public school so far as secular studies were concerned, besides providing in it a training of heart and will that would conduce very materially to good citizenship. All his life after this he was devoted to the thought of making parochial schools just as efficient as possible and that came to be one of the tasks that he took most to heart during the time that he was archbishop and cardinal. Feeling that purely secular education unless associated with religious training leaves people without a firm anchorage in life, he was sure that the best contribution the Catholic Church could make for good citizenship in America was to provide that combination of religious and secular studies which trained the whole man and not merely his intellect at the expense of his will.

It is only with the rise of the next generation so many of them entirely without religious training that the increase in the amount of crime and the looseness of living have asserted themselves which are gradually waking up this generation to the realization of the foresight of men like Cardinal Farley when they devoted themselves to the development to the utmost of religious schools here in America. It is only in our own day that we have come to realize that knowledge alone may actually be harmful rather than beneficial to mankind. If education does not make men better it may serve only to make clever scoundrels and there are too many criminals

in our prisons and any number more outside of them
which show us that universal education alone does
not make men better unless it develops their heart
as well as their head, that is, increases the sum total
of kindly impulses in them. "Where these kindly
impulses exist," as Bertrand Russell said, "science
helps them to be effective; where they are absent,
science only makes men more cleverly diabolic."
No wonder then that the Cardinal Archbishop of
New York felt that his life work could not be better
directed than to making religious schools just as
efficient as possible both intellectually and morally.
His emphasis on this point accomplished wonders in
the raising up of parochial schools to the position
which they occupy at the present time but above
all for the future of development that is planned
for them.

Cardinal Farley himself in later life used to say
that the most useful period of his life so far as his
own personal development was concerned came as
the result of the years as pastor of St. Gabriel's
Church. It brought him into intimate contact with
both priests and people and above all it taught him
the duties, the opportunities, the trials and the joys
of a pastor's work. Nothing could have been better
for him as a preparation for the higher ecclesiastical
duties that he was destined to fulfill. He organized

the spiritual side of his parish, saw that its religious societies of various kinds flourished, not alone in numbers but in spirit, and brought the priests and people ever closer together. From the practical side of the pastor's life he learned much that was of value for the administration of his diocese. He was always very practical minded and his parish was a model of administration. He freed the church from debt and had it consecrated, which is not permitted by the church authorities until the last dollar of indebtedness has been paid on the property. In preparation for this event he had finished the spire of the church and renovated its whole interior.

It might be thought that he would stop after this and consider that his work was done and that others might bring about any further developments and that as it were something should be left for his successor to do. Monsignor Farley however built the parish hall so as to have a meeting place for his parishioners and to bring about more intimate contact among them. He felt that above all it was extremely important to bring Catholic young folk together in various festivities for thus they learned to know each other and marriages within the household of the faith were more likely to occur. The mixed marriage evil is one of lack of opportunities for Catholic young folks to meet while social op-

portunities for the meeting with those outside of
the Church are so abundant. After this he planned
the erection of a new school and it was only his
call to higher duties that made him leave this work
for his successor though under such circumstances
as made it incumbent on that successor to fulfill his
duty. Monsignor Farley also during his pastorship
at St. Gabriel's instituted parochial visitation by the
clergy of all the members of the parish in order that
there might be closer touch between priests and
people and even the least of those committed to his
care might not be neglected through any fault of
his. It was to this devoted pastor of his people that
there came as the reward for his zealous labors
though all unlooked for, the promotion to the position of Auxiliary Bishop of New York. No appointment could have been more felicitous nor more welcome to priests and people.

The first incident to call attention to the future
cardinal's influence with the priests and people of
the New York archdiocese, occurred in connection
with the celebration of the silver jubilee of Archbishop Corrigan's elevation to the rank of bishop in
1898. As Auxiliary Bishop of New York he consulted with the leading priests as to the most satisfactory token of affection and loyalty that they could
give the archbishop on the occasion. The new St.

Joseph's Seminary at Dunwoodie which had been completed some two years before was still burdened with a debt of $300,000. Thirty years ago this seemed a very large sum, and the lifting of it would probably prove a source of more relief for the archbishop than anything else that could be done. Bishop Farley undertook the leadership of the movement and carried it to complete success. On May 4, 1898, the day of the celebration, the mortgage was burned and the satisfaction piece was placed in the hands of the happy and grateful archbishop. That seemed a magnificent financial feat in those days when war experience had not taught people to "give until it hurts" and when we were not yet used to thinking in billions but only in millions and hundreds of thousands represented a very large amount.

Very probably the most profound interest in Cardinal Farley's heart was for Catholic education. In 1891 on the death of Monsignor Preston, Monsignor Farley was named as vicar general. In this position he became president of the Catholic School Board and devoted much of his time and a very large proportion of his energy to the work of making the Catholic schools just as efficient as possible. He had already had experience in his own parish of St. Gabriel's in the reorganization and systematization of the parochial school and now he had the whole field of the archdiocese to labor in to similar purpose.   He felt that even Catholics themselves did not appreciate how much Catholicity in New York was doing for Catholic school work. Accordingly the year after he became president of the Catholic School Board he organized the Catholic School parade (1892) which was a revelation to New Yorkers of all classes and quite as much to Catholics as to those outside of the Church.   Two years later, in 1894, he organized a Catholic School exhibit which produced an even profounder impression because this showed not only the numbers that were being influenced by Catholic education but also the mode of that influence and how thoroughgoing it was.   After this Catholics felt justly prouder of our school system and non-Catholics came to realize that here indeed was a determined successful effort to conjoin religious training with development of the intelligence by means of secular study.

What Cardinal Farley accomplished for Catholic education is briefly and succinctly reviewed by Right Reverend Monsignor Lavelle in his sketch of Cardinal Farley (Paulist Press, 1919).   As Monsignor Lavelle was one of those closest to Cardinal Farley during his life, an associate in many of his activities, this paragraph may be taken as an authentic summary of the cardinal's relations to education. "He (Cardinal Farley) was impregnated with the conviction that Catholic education is the greatest of all evangelizing forces, and he fostered everything that promised to strengthen and diffuse Catholic scholarship. In fair weather and foul he was a firm believer in and an unflinching friend of the Catholic University in Washington. He followed with interest the meetings and the proceedings of the Catholic National Education Association. He encouraged the colleges and high schools in his own diocese. He caused the erection of fifty new schools, and doubled during his administration the number of children studying in them. His respect and love for the children was so great, that he never allowed an important celebration to pass without having a special Mass sung and attended by the children and their teachers, alone. He assigned his senior Vicar General to the presidency of the Catholic School Board; caused monthly meetings to be held; and provided competent superintendents for the regular visitation, inspection and examination of every school. He also was the father of 'The Workers for God and Country,' an association of Catholic public-school teachers, two thousand in number, for the religious education of the children of newly-arrived foreign people, who had been unreached by either the Catholic day schools or Sunday-schools."

Cardinal Farley's one ambition as Archbishop of New York, which he became in September, 1902, was to make his archdiocese just as perfect an organic member of the Catholic Church as it could be made. He had no ulterior ambition. He cared little for personal prestige. He wanted to feel that he was fulfilling the duties which devolved upon him just as perfectly as possible. His personality was so attractive that he won men to second his efforts very cordially. When he succeeded to the archbishopric of New York it was rent with disunion and feuds among the clergy because of unfortunate divisions of opinion on certain political and economic questions. Under his predecessor these had grown more divisive as time went on. Archbishop Farley soon proved an ideal appeaser of the troubles.

He felt that a number of the clergy who had been in disagreement with his predecessor were deeply conscientious in their conduct and had been supported by the best of motives. He knew all of them personally quite well and he felt that many of them had done such thoroughgoing work for the Church that instead of anything like ecclesiastical censure they rather deserved ecclesiastical preferment. He felt that such preferment by rewarding them for the past would make them more zealous in efforts for the Church's glory and benefit in the future. On one of his early visits to Rome then as Archbishop of New York he asked and obtained from the Pope a series of monsignorates for these older men of his diocese. The monsignorial dignity was not as familiar in America at that time as it has since become. Indeed it was Cardinal Farley's recognition of the fact that pastors of long and faithful service deserved some such official recognition that properly introduced the dignity into the American Church. Probably no one was half so much surprised at the ecclesiastical honors which were accorded as some of the men to whom they came, for not a few of them had the feeling that they were not in favor with their ecclesiastical superiors though they had undoubtedly tried to do their duty as they saw it. This recognition of their good faith and faithful service in pastoral duty won them over and made a new era in the history of the archdiocese of New York.

It was when these new *monsignori* blossomed out in all the effulgence of their purple rabbis that his grace, the Archbishop of Philadelphia, the irrepressible Archbishop O'Ryan, with a humorous twinkle in his eye said to his grace of New York, "I understand, your grace, that since your recent visit to

Rome half of your diocese has become purple and the other half blue." Jokes of this kind in ecclesiastical matters are supposed by some religious-minded people to be scarcely in good taste. Religion is supposed to be a very serious thing. No one would appreciate however better the humor in the expression and the humorous twinkle in the eye of his colleague of Philadelphia than Archbishop Farley. Catholic churchmen are very prone to see the humor of situations. Indeed no set of men that I know appreciates humor better than they do. It is perfectly possible to take religion too seriously. Man is a risible animal, in a certain sense at least, is as good a definition as that he is a rational animal. The very use of reason demands that we shall see the incongruities of things which constitute the basis of human nature, that combination of animal and spiritual elements that makes man so incongruous a creature in many ways. This often seems hard for people to understand who think that religion is a very solemn affair and that religious dignitaries must be constantly in serious mood. To know Catholic prelates even a little intimately is to be persuaded that quiet humor and religion go hand in hand. Horace's dictum, *ridentem dicere vera quid vetat*— to smile and tell the truth what harm?—might well be the motto of many a Catholic bishop. In no one was this better exemplified than in Cardinal Farley, and he could be humorous himself and enjoy the humor of others thoroughly.

As archbishop, John Farley proved to be not only public spirited but internationally minded. Probably the most striking demonstration of this is to be found in the immense mass meeting which he organized in New York in 1905 at the Hippodrome in order to make a determined protest against the persecutory laws which the French Parliament were at that time striving to impose upon the Church in France. On that occasion the immense auditorium of the Hippodrome was thronged even beyond its capacity so that there was some solicitude over the numbers who were packed into it, but more than six times as many, calculated to be over 30,000, tried to get in for the meeting. The protests made by some of the most distinguished laymen specially chosen from among the representative Catholics of New York City were thoroughly dignified but eminently forcible and carried a great deal of moral weight with them. The newspaper reports of the meeting were large and details of it were published all over the world. There is no doubt at all that these produced an almost immediate effect and probably put an end to further legislation along the same line and even modified the application of such laws as had been passed so that they were not carried out with the rigor that would otherwise almost inevitably have been exercised. The Roman authorities recognized that here had been a worthy exercise of episcopal prudence and influence in America carried out with devoted zeal yet pregnant with excellent effect for the cause of the Church.

Cardinal Farley's influence in the preliminary movement for the bringing out of the *Catholic Encyclopedia* and above all his cordial patronage and sympathy during the progress of the work did much to make that work the magnificent success that it was. It was not until after he had called a meeting in his own house at which he strongly endorsed the project, himself pledged $5,000 and called for subscriptions, that it became perfectly clear that a definite beginning had been made. That gave the signal for the holding of meetings in other dioceses at which subscriptions were taken so generously that there could be no further doubt of the success of the work.

All during the course of its publication as the archbishop of the diocese in which the work was published Cardinal Farley continued his hearty approval. He showed such confidence in the editors and such eagerness to facilitate their purposes that he actually constituted them their own censors.

This was all the more noteworthy because at the moment there were rather serious dicussions sometimes rising to the plane of bitter disputes over matters of doctrine and even the most correct writers were sometimes in danger of being considered incorrect if not un-Catholic in their statements. After all it may be well to recall that terms in theology often come to have a modification of meaning that sometimes makes them seem to convey a very different significance from what was intended by the writer. As a result of this even the greatest theologians of the Church have sometimes had to make corrections and additions and even Doctors of the Church have for a time been under condemnation through no fault of theirs.

Cardinal Farley trusted the editors of the *Encyclopedia* in this regard so absolutely that even when in order to reassure correctness of doctrine in every particular the Holy See instructed the bishops of the Catholic world to appoint committees for this purpose in their dioceses, His Eminence of New York still left it to the judgment and discretion of the editors to determine what articles were to be submitted to this committee. Any one who knows how difficult a matter the editorship of a great encyclopedia is will appreciate at once how much this largeness of sympathy with the editors and his unswerving confidence in them facilitated their great work which was crowned with such eminent success. His noble conception of the work and his complete reliance on the editors under such difficult conditions was an extraordinarily broad and brave thing to do and amply deserves that the cardinal should be thought of as the founder of the *Catholic Encyclopedia*.

No one was prouder of the achievement than he when it was completed. It represented an extraordinary marshaling of the scholarship of the Catholic Church throughout the world that made the English-speaking peoples understand better than ever before the greatness of the old Church. Practically every bishop in every English-speaking country, and over a thousand scholars, priests and laymen, in forty-three different countries coöperated in the production of this work. As Goyau, the distinguished French *litterateur* said of it, "It marshalled the Catholic intellectual forces of the modern world, as the Crusades had marshalled the Catholic military forces of the Middle Ages." How much of this is owed to Cardinal Farley and the breadth of his sympathy with the work and his largeness of mind and fearlessness of purpose should be recognized by all.

In his position as Archbishop of New York he

was a magnificent organizer. As one who was closest to him said, "He was aided in this by a keen sense of the importance of great occasions." He knew when and how to make an appeal to his people to show their enthusiastic fidelity to the Church and when he called upon them to exhibit their loyalty he met with a marvelous response. In 1908 occurred the Centenary of the diocese of New York. It might very well have been observed merely as a New York affair but that would not satisfy Archbishop Farley and he saw how much of an opportunity there was in it to make his people realize the progress that had been made in a hundred years and still more the present position of the Church. He put a touch of internationalism into it that at once attracted attention by inviting Cardinal Logue, Archbishop of Armagh and direct successor of St. Patrick, the prelate in whose archdiocese the cardinal himself had been born, to come to New York to celebrate the Mass and to be the honored guest of the occasion. Nothing could have been more appropriate than that this occupant of the See of St. Patrick in our day should now grace with his presence the celebration of a hundred years of Church life in this great diocese of the West, whose cathedral was under the invocation of the great apostle of the Irish.

The festivities in connection with the celebration lasted a full week, every day of which had its special observance and its appeal to some special class in the Catholic community. The religious were invited to come to the Cathedral, the children had their day, and the priests theirs. The celebration closed with a laymen's parade in which many of the next day's newspapers declared that some 50,000 men were in line. New York had probably never witnessed a procession the equal of this for impressiveness. The route of the procession was lined with Catholics and non-Catholics many rows deep to see this testimony on the part of New York Catholic gentlemen to their great archdiocese and its head. Such events produce a much wider effect than might be thought in making people reflect upon the place of the Church in American life and above all in strengthening the faith of those who have any part in the celebration, and in reviving the faith of those on whom modern materialistic thought and the sordid interests of life have brought some eclipse of their loyalty and adhesion to the Church.

After a triumph like this it might seem as though the archbishop would prudently rest on the laurels of such a success and leave to other men opportunities to rival it in the future. Only two years later however Archbishop Farley planned the celebration of the consecration of the cathedral in 1910 and if possible attracted even more attention than the celebration of the Centenary. On this occasion he invited the Holy Father, the Pope, to be represented by special delegate and Cardinal Vanutelli, one of the most important members of the Papal Curia came to America to celebrate the Mass with Cardinals Gibbons and Logue present in the sanctuary, during the celebration. This occasion which might have been scarcely more than a family matter for the priests of the diocese and the people of the cathedral parish came as a result to take on almost an international aspect and attracted national attention throughout the United States. The effect on Catholics was noteworthy and made them feel that they were members of a great American branch of the Apostolic Church with recognition from all over the world accorded to them though only a generation before they had represented scarcely more than a very small minority of the poorer people of the country.

Six years later, when in 1916 the Federation of Catholic Societies of the United States held its convention in New York City once more Archbishop Farley, now cardinal, as he was not in preceding celebrations, insisted on the organization of a magnificent Church welcome for them. This took the form of a High Mass celebrated by himself in the presence of Cardinals Gibbons and O'Connell and the greater part of the bishops of the United States, together with the representatives of the Papal Knights of St. Gregory from many parts of the country. The great mass meeting in Madison Square Garden at which the three cardinals and the governor of the state of New York made addresses followed by distinguished Catholic laymen will always be remembered for its magnitude and enthusiasm. The Garden was crowded to its utmost limit of capacity but there were nearly as many more who had come in the vain hope that there might be some chance in so large a place to find entrance and there were literally tens of thousands of others who would have made the effort to attend the meeting if they had the slightest inkling that there would be a chance for admission. In affairs of this kind Cardinal Farley's power of organization was superb and assured success that reflected honor and dignity on the occasion.

It was no wonder then that taking a leaf out of their archbishop's book when in 1911 he was elevated to the cardinalate, others should plan to give him a worthy celebration on his home-coming from Rome after his investment with the insignia of his high office. He arrived in New York January

18, 1912.   He was received at the pier by the
leading clergy and laity of his diocese.   They led
a procession to welcome him which accompanied him
to his cathedral.   As the procession passed up
Broadway and Fifth Avenue the streets were lined
for a distance of four miles with thronging multi-
tudes whose ringing cheers gave testimony at once
of their enthusiastic joy over his advancement but
also of their intense affection for their own archbishop whom they had learned to love so dearly.
All the buildings, public and private, on the way and
all the churches were decorated in honor of the
occasion.   The streets adjoining the cathedral were
packed with people who joined heartily in the glad
Te Deum that was intoned for his safe return wear-
ing his new dignity.   The cathedral itself was
crowded to capacity and the most careful regulations had to be made to keep it from being jammed
by the crowds who wished to enter.   Every night
for a week the exterior of the cathedral was illuminated with electric lights which brought out the
beautiful lines of the great Gothic structure and led
the eye upwards to the crosses pointing heavenward
that crowned its spires.

This was however only the beginning of the celebration.   Some two weeks later, January 25th, his
formal installation as cardinal took place in the

cathedral in the presence of the Apostolic Delegate, the papal representative in this country, Cardinal Gibbons and some sixty of the most important members of the American hierarchy. The same night there was a great reception at the Catholic Club attended by the élite among the Catholics of the city; probably one of the greatest affairs that the Club has ever witnessed. On the following Sunday night a more public demonstration to which thousands of Catholics crowded from all over the city, was given at the Hippodrome. Each one of these events seemed to surpass the other in the éclat which it evoked and made it very clear that here indeed was a man whom the people of New York City loved to honor.

But what must be considered as very probably the most remarkable feature of the entire celebration of the return of the cardinal from Rome remains to be recorded. It consisted of a magnificent public dinner which was tendered to him at the Waldorf-Astoria Hotel not by his own people this time but by prominent non-Catholics. The toastmaster of this occasion was Hon. Herman A. Metz, Comptroller of the City. Addresses were made by the Governor of New York State, by Mayor Gaynor of New York City, by the Hon. John Finley, State Commissioner of Education, and by Hon. Oscar S.

Straus, Secretary of Commerce and Labor in the Cabinet of President Roosevelt. The affair was a magnificent success and attracted the attention of the nation once more to the Archbishop of New York and the loyalty of his people. It is very probable that the series of events connected with his home-coming as cardinal represents beyond doubt the most wonderful demonstration ever made by the American metropolis in honor of any individual. Every element of New York City's people and every political party of importance was represented in cordial dignified greeting to this great churchman whose tender feelings not only for his own people but for the country and its citizens everywhere were so well-known.

President Taft sent a letter of regret that he could not owing to circumstances over which he had no control take a part in the celebration. He wrote: "I regret I am unable to be present at the dinner to Cardinal Farley on his elevation to the highest rank of the Roman Catholic Church. The non-sectarian character of the dinner is an indication of the great progress we have made in mutual tolerance and brotherly coöperation. Please present my compliments to Cardinal Farley, with whose friendship I have been honored for many years."

While it is not generally known, Cardinal Farley

even during the period while he was Archbishop of
New York made the time—no other phrase ade-
quately expresses the special effort that must have
been required—to do so in the midst of his many
duties, to write the *History of St. Patrick's Cathedral* (New York, 1908).   Then years later while
he was cardinal he wrote chiefly as a labor of love
and reverence *The Life of Cardinal McCloskey*
(New York, 1918), his distinguished predecessor
in the combined positions of archbishop and cardinal.
These books illustrate very well his patient devotion to any work that he took in hand, his thoroughness, his simplicity and lack of anything like pre-
tentiousness.   The volume *The Life of Cardinal
McCloskey* is really a valuable contribution to the
biographical studies of the Catholic churchmen of
America that bring out the place of the Catholic
Church in the history of the United States during
the second half of the nineteenth century.   It was
written as a labor of love in the midst of onerous
duties of the archiepiscopate by one who had been
himself a participant in some of the activities and
who knew at first hand from those who had most
to do with them and especially from Cardinal
McCloskey himself the underlying significance of
a great many of the events that are narrated.   It
makes a precious collection of data for the historian

of the Church but also for the general historian who will come to recognize something of the importance of the rôle played by the Catholic Church and her ecclesiastics in the life of the country during this period.

While Cardinal Farley was so deeply intent on the thoroughgoing organization of his own diocese and on making it just as far as possible a perfect ecclesiastical organization, he was not narrow in his interests and above all he was not limited in his charity toward other great Church movements apart from those of his diocese. He recalled with the most ardent gratitude the benefits that had been conferred upon America and the struggling Church in the United States by the missionary efforts of other countries and above all by the money contributions that came to struggling Catholic communities in the United States from distant peoples. South America early in the history of Catholicity in the United States actually contributed many thousands of dollars for the support of Catholic missionaries and the building of Catholic churches in the cities of this country. Many European peoples had done the same thing and had continued to make their contributions until the Catholic Church in America was well organized and could maintain itself without difficulty. Cardinal Farley felt that we

owed a deep debt of gratitude to other countries
for this reason and that we should repay it in the
days of our prosperity as lavishly as we could so
well afford, now that our country was becoming
one of the richest in the world.

There is an organization in the Church known
as the Society for the Propagation of the Faith
whose purpose is to collect money in various countries where the zeal and charity of the faithful
prompt them to fulfill their duty of contributing to
the support of missions in pagan countries or in
localities where the poverty of Catholics makes it
very difficult for them to support their own priests
and church organizations.   Cardinal Farley took
this Society particularly under his protection and
devoted the heartiest attention to making it accomplish its purposes in a way worthy of this great
country of ours.   Contributions to the Society for
the Propagation of the Faith in New York used to
consist of a few thousand dollars annually, before
his time and even this was considered to represent
a generous interest on the part of our people.   It
seemed to Cardinal Farley entirely too small a contribution considering our wealth and the memories
of old-time contributions made to us, so much more
liberally. As the result of his interest, the sum raised
for the Society for the Propagation of the Faith rose

constantly during his years as archbishop until the New York contribution in 1918 was more than a quarter of a million of dollars. Even with this he felt that our contributions had not reached the limit but must continue to advance with the further growth of the city and the Catholic population of the archdiocese.

He did not stop with this in his interest in the missions however nor feel that a triumph of this kind ought to be sufficient index of his interest in the propagation of the faith outside of his diocese. He loved to greet missionaries who came from a distance and gave them every opportunity to collect funds in his diocese. So far from thinking that money contributed to the missionaries would be just that much taken from contributions that might be made to parish or diocesan funds, he was quite convinced that the habit of giving, thus fostered, would even add to regular contributions, but that above all a blessing from on High would help out the work of the diocesan clergy as a result of the communication of the spirit of the missionaries to priests and people so that the greatest possible benefit would redound to the Church. He often said that he felt that nothing could be better for the spiritual side of Catholicity in our country than to be brought in intimate contact with the spirit of

self-sacrifice and intense devotion of every power of
heart and soul that characterized missionary efforts.
He was sure that he saw actual signs of the production of such an effect, of edification and intensifica-
tion of faith that resulted therefrom, hence his ever
increasing readiness to welcome the missionaries and
give them such material aid as he could.

When that modern apostle, Father James A.
Walsh, the founder of the Catholic Foreign Mission Society proposed to establish the mother house
of his organization at Maryknoll near Ossining in
the New York archdiocese, Cardinal Farley received
him with open arms, encouraged him in every way,
and provided ample assurance that New York would
surely make its success certain. In the early struggling days the cardinal helped it in every way,
above all by his personal interest, and he must surely
be recalled as a very important factor for its wonderful success. There is no institution in the archdiocese of which Catholics who know as much about
it as they should are prouder than the great missionary institution of Maryknoll which is sending its
dozens of priests and sisters to Korea and China
during these recent years. We hear much of the
Yellow Peril but one thing is perfectly sure that
when the Chinese people wake up, as inevitably they
must before long, to become a factor in modern civi-

lization, it will be an extremely valuable benefit for our western civilization that these missionary priests and sisters from the archdiocese of New York have been for years working to make Christianity better understood by the Chinese and to make the fundamental principles of Christian civilization intelligible to them.

All his life Cardinal Farley continued to be a man of the spirit and of prayer. He urged his people to the practice of devotion of various kinds but he was above all one who first did and then asked that others should do. He urged frequent Holy Communion, visits to the Blessed Sacrament and devotion to the Sacred Heart and the Blessed Virgin as the surest signs of devout Catholic faith, but also as the surest means of obtaining ever increase of devotion. It was well-known that he himself set a very edifying example in this regard and those who were close to him were well aware that in times of trial and difficulty he turned for help and strength and enlightenment to the Master.

Above all he felt that the prayers of others could be of great help to him and that is said to be the supreme test of faith in prayer. He favored the foundation of chapels of perpetual adoration, that is of places where devout women succeed each other from hour to hour all during the day and the night praying for the benefit not only of the Church but of the country. He added to the number of these chapels and was always ready to welcome further additions to the contemplative orders feeling that while the religious who do the practical work of the Church are of very great importance, the success of their work and of the efforts of the clergy and their archbishop are dependent on prayer. He believed with St. Ignatius that while men should work as if everything depended on them, they should pray as if everything depended on God and then leave all to Him. Hence it was that Cardinal Farley tried to make his diocese just as far as possible a place of prayer and he ordered that all churches should be opened during the entire day and until nine o'clock at night.

He believed that the success of his archdiocese depended to the greatest possible extent on the spiritual progress of his priests. He insisted therefore that all of them should make retreats annually. As there were a number of Italian priests who could not understand English, he arranged that they should have a separate retreat by themselves and he tried as far as possible to enhance the interior religious life of all the foreign-speaking priests of his diocese.

He instituted what is called the Monthly Recollection. On the last Tuesday of each month all the priests of his diocese were invited to Cathedral College situated on the block just north of the cathedral, for a spiritual conference followed by Benediction of the Blessed Sacrament. He saw to it that these spiritual conferences were of very high order and were given by men who could be depended on to lift up the hearts of those who heard them and renew their interior spirit. These Monthly Recollections he made it a point always to attend himself whenever he was in his diocese and was very careful that as far as possible his engagements elsewhere should not interfere with this simple regular duty as he considered it to be. He attended not only for the sake of the example that was thus given, but manifestly because he felt that he himself needed such an awakening of the spirit and that he was benefited by it. These Monthly Recollections beyond their immediate benefit became a strong link between the priests and himself and afforded an opportunity for him to speak to them with regard to any topic that might be of importance at the time.

It was arrangements of this kind that made his priests feel deeply his tender paternal solicitude for them and his desire to make them just as perfect instruments as possible for the fulfillment of their religious work. The morale thus engendered among the clergy was excellent for its effect upon them as men and as priests. The result was a unanimity of heart and soul, *cor unum et anima una,* such as is very seldom seen, particularly where such large numbers of individuals are concerned. It was Cardinal Farley's own spirit shared with his priests that brought about this thoroughgoing concord in the diocese.

Cardinal Farley was personally a very happy man. He had the faculty of picking out men for certain responsibilities leaving them absolutely to those responsibilities and insisting on regular reports which kept him in touch with their work. There was no tincture of worrisomeness in his disposition. No one was more meticulously careful of the administrative obligations of his great diocese and no one more punctiliously prompt in attendance at meetings of committees and councils and he insisted on the same punctuality from others so that sometimes he was considered a martinet in the matter, but it was this very definite attention to details that lessened the burdens of all. His constantly cheery disposition to quote the words of his closest official in the diocese, "radiated its brightness on all with whom he came in contact. He took a special pleasure in his relations with his official

family to whom he was strongly attached and which
returned his affection with cheerful and never fail-
ing loyalty." To know him well was to be able to
say that here was a man who had found his work
and he had the blessedness of those who have found
their work. With all this he was a first-class business man, one who in civil life might have been a
captain of industry.

His administration of his great archdiocese was
of a character that united it wonderfully for the
fulfillment of the Christian work for which it was
organized. He introduced the practice that all the
priests should have their first parish and experience
of parochial work in one of the country districts
around New York and after a reasonable period of
service under rural conditions be promoted to city
positions. This served two excellent purposes.
First, the country parishes were given the benefit of
the very highest talent to the great advantage of
the people of the rural districts. But secondly, the
practice was very advantageous for the clergy themselves, for they learned their pastoral duties in the
less complex conditions of the country parishes and
yet had to go through some of the trials and difficulties that are more or less inevitable in connection
with smaller parish work. This trained them in
character for their city work and proved a sort of

novitiate for the responsibilities of the large city parishes that were to come to them later. It was a source of great satisfaction to the priests themselves since it made them feel that every one had to go through this routine which was at once educational in mind and edifying in heart and soul and represented a real formation of character that made for their appropriate development as priests.

The question of the care of the foreigners in his archdiocese was one which appealed strongly to Cardinal Farley. After all, there are spoken in the archdiocese of New York more tongues than are recorded in the Scriptures on the day of Pentecost and above all the eastern peoples have drifted into the American metropolis to constitute colonies of various sizes in the different parts of the city. Perhaps nothing will bring the diversity of these home to Catholics as well as Protestants more than the fact that though the Mass is usually said to be said in Latin in the Catholic Church, it is well-known that altogether nine languages may be used by various peoples in their liturgies, all of them under the ægis of the Pope. Of these nine different languages in which the Mass may be said, no less than seven are actually in use in New York. All these people have to have religious services provided for them in their own tongues and with the liturgies to which they are accustomed in their native countries. Cardinal Farley created special committees for the intensive and particular care of the newly arrived foreign peoples. This redounded to the great spiritual benefit of the people and of the diocese as well as of the city and country, for all of these strange foreign people were brought under the conservative influence of the Church just at the time when their new sense of liberty and independence consequent upon their living in a free country might have brought them under the sway of anarchistic tendencies or of socialistic and communistic demagogues, ever ready to find followers among the newly arrived peoples in order to increase their own importance politically and socially.

Cardinal Farley's efforts were especially directed toward the care of the Italians for he had himself lived in Italy for years, knew the language well and was thoroughly sympathetic with the Italian people. Owing to political disturbances in Italy and the hampering of Church activities in the peninsula during the past generation, a great many of the Italians who came to this country were weak-kneed in the practice of their faith and needed to be cared for especially to keep them from drifting into infidelity. Nearly a million of Italian immigrants settled in New York during the last decade of the nineteenth century and soon began to multiply rapidly so that the Italian problem in the New York archdiocese became a very serious one. At the time of Cardinal Farley's death the demonstration of how well he had reached the practical solution of the Italian question was to be found in the fact that there were nearly fifty Italian churches in the archdiocese, all of them self-supporting and improving in their hold upon the people in every way.

The last years of his life ran parallel with the Great War that was devastating civilization at the end of the first quarter of the twentieth century. Just as soon as the United States entered the War, Cardinal Farley proceeded to exercise every possible effort in order to be helpful to the country in its great purpose of making the world safe for democracy and finishing triumphantly the War that it was hoped would end war for all time. He nominated immediately after the declaration of war a New York Catholic War Council to second every patriotic effort and to provide help of any and every kind for war needs. The Council held its meetings every week. It accomplished a number of very laudable purposes. It opened the Cardinal Farley Soldiers' and Sailors' Club in 30th Street, the Young Women's Catholic Patriotic Club on Lexington Avenue, the Catholic Hospital for Shell Shocked

Patients. It also provided means for the extension
of the League of Catholic Women and furnished
efficient workers and afforded substantial financial
aid to at least a dozen other war activities in the
more or less immediate neighborhood of New York
City. Had the War continued these activities would
have been very much broadened and rendered still
more efficient, and the Cardinal himself was the soul
of them all, and though he was now a man past
seventy-five he was ready to spend the last spark of
energy for the benefit of his adopted country. Indeed his efforts to be of help to the American cause
probably shortened his life.

His attitude of thoroughgoing loyalty toward the
United States government was demonstrated very
clearly when after so many well meant efforts on the
part of our President to keep us out of the War
we were at last plunged into it. Rev. Dr. Guilday
in his brief sketch of the cardinal written shortly
after his death which appeared in the *Catholic
World* for November, 1918 (beside the sketch of
Archbishop Ireland written by Rev. Dr. Humphrey
Moynihan, for the two great prelates died that same
year in the same month and almost in the same
week) told in a single paragraph Cardinal Farley's
war attitude. When this paragraph was written we
were still in the midst of the War and it was not

sure but that the War would last at least until the following year. Rev. Dr. Guilday quotes the cardinal's saying, "We are fighting to uphold those ideals of political liberty and freedom which guarantee to every nation, great and small, peaceful possession of its territory, unhampered development of natural resources and equal opportunity in industrial and commercial competition."

Rev. Dr. Guilday, who in connection with historical studies referring to the archdiocese of New York had been very close to Cardinal Farley during many years while the cardinal was getting together the material for his life of Cardinal McCloskey, adds a comment on the cardinal's patriotism that deserves to be noted because the writer knew so well the mind of the cardinal from intimate association with him. He said, "His constant prayer from the day that America entered the conflict was that the God of battles would give us justice, freedom and peace. John, Cardinal Farley stood for everything that America is fighting for—for the restoration of honor and rectitude among the nations of the earth; for the right of small nations in the pursuit of their own self-determination; for the emancipation of oppressed peoples; for responsibility in government."

Very few people outside the Church had any real

conception of the greatness of Cardinal Farley's work. If there was anything in the world that he did not care for it was notoriety or what has come to be called publicity. While others crave so much he was not only utterly negligent of it but took every possible precaution to avoid it. He avoided praise and as Monsignor Lavelle said of him, "During his sixteen years as Archbishop of New York, he was probably never criticised in the public press notwithstanding that every day of his life was full of activity." Almost needless to say this can be said of very few men who occupy a public position of any kind and it is the best possible testimony to Cardinal Farley's prudence of administration and his practical wisdom. No wonder that a well-known writer for the public press not over given to encomiums, said of him the day after his death, "Cardinal Farley was a man perfectly fitted for his position."

What Monsignor Lavelle says of him, "There is not a faction nor a clique in the diocese he left behind," is only another index of the whole-heartedness of the man, the breadth of his sympathies, the depth of his humanity, and the testimony that it all provides for the inevitable conclusion that "here indeed was a man."

WILLIAM, CARDINAL O'CONNELL

FOURTH AMERICAN CARDINAL

WILLIAM, CARDINAL O'CONNELL, Archbishop of Boston, was born December 8, 1859 at Lowell in Massachusetts, the seventh son and the eleventh child in a large Irish family. The cardinal is a striking example of that truth so little appreciated in our day that a great many of the men who reached distinction in the past were born late in families. Physicians who have looked into the matter rather carefully declare that the later children in families when father and mother are both healthy are usually more stable in mental equilibrium, often physically stronger and not rarely have more acute intellectuality than the early born children. A good many of the geniuses of the world have been born after the fifth in the family and it has even been suggested that one of the reasons why real genius, by which is not meant mere talent nor cleverness, is so much rarer in proportion to the population than it was generations ago, is that to a great extent we are missing the ends of the families. Marriage is

CARDINAL O'CONNELL

delayed, children are fewer and the best human products are not secured.

The cardinal's parents had both been born in Ireland and were married over there and their first six children were born there. His mother, Bridget Farley, was raised in the charming little village of Enagh in County Cavan, where she came from a prosperous, landowning family. His father, John O'Connell, came of a well-known old family of the County Meath, though his branch of it was not wealthy. The young folks met and were married in Enagh and established their household there. When already they had six children conditions of living in Ireland became almost impossible. The famine years followed the failure of the potato crop, for lack of food and because of lowered resistive vitality a murrain came over the cattle, and the future looked blank indeed. Their hearts were in their little home in Enagh which by this time had so many family memories clustering round it, but for the sake of their children's future they decided to tear themselves loose from these home ties and emigrate to America. The sadness of such partings from the homeland is very little appreciated as an element in the lives of the Irish who thus bravely turned their faces toward the setting sun because nothing was too much to do for their children's sake.

Lowell, Massachusetts, was selected as the site of their home in the new world because they had relatives there who had often invited them to come over to the United States for the sake of the prospects that were held out before their children. Besides, the bitterness of parting from home it was no little job for a mother to take six little ones across the ocean to a strange land, especially in the vessels of those days, but Mrs. O'Connell faced the trial bravely. It proved a good discipline for some harder tasks that were ahead of her in their adopted country. She did not flinch at the prospect.

They were able to buy a pretty cottage with a little garden, an extremely suitable place for bringing up their growing boys and soon other children were added to the family. Mother had a very busy time managing in her gentle lovable way all her children and was the head of the house. Father was a quiet man without much ambition, a student and a dreamer, who would sit over in a corner with a book and read after his day's work was done. Mother's powerful personality asserted itself and on a very limited income she was able to bring up a family of eleven children and give them all the advantages of a liberal education. Her seven boys still worship the memory of her and realize how much they owe to her both by heredity and her example of indomitable courage.

Father fell ill and was for months confined to his room and in those days when there were no trained nurses this added still more to mother's tasks. At the age of fifty-six John O'Connell died. The future cardinal only four years old was roused from his sleep one night by an older sister and crept down stairs to his parents' bedroom to see the body of his dead father lying on the bed and kneeling beside it, her face buried in the pillows, his heart-broken mother murmuring "God's Will be done." The older brothers and sisters were gathered round her repeating mother's words. This is the first recollection of His Eminence's life.

Mother had to face the future for herself and her orphan children and every one had to help to the best of his or her ability. Education was the watchword in the family and William was sent to school in the old Edson School, a red brick structure on one corner of the South Common in Lowell which is still in use. In five years he finished his grammar school studies but attracted no particular attention and did not stand at the head of his class or anywhere near it. His mother wanted him to have a high-school training and he entered high school with a dread in his heart, for he looked forward to a repetition of monotonous grammar-shool days. This was all changed by contact with Professor Edwin Lord, the teacher of chemistry, who had a genius for teaching. This was the first person outside his family who deeply impressed himself on his life, who gave him an impetus and an inspiration for study for which he retains a lifelong gratitude. Still when the cardinal talks of him he says a fervent "God bless him" for this teacher.

As a consequence of his interest in chemistry the future cardinal felt himself drawn toward medicine as a profession but the decision of that question was in the future. That was the practical side of him but there was another side, that of the dreamer inherited from his father, and during one summer vacation he chanced to read Bryant's "Thanatopsis." He had read it often before in connection with his high-school work but now for the first time he realized its poetic beauty. It thrilled him. He went home amazed and delighted with the new vista opening before him. It has continued to be ever since his favorite poem, often quoted from. It opened up the world of books for him.

After his graduation from high school the thought of becoming a priest came to him and though he felt poignantly his own unworthiness he decided to enter St. Charles College in Maryland where young men were trained for the priesthood. The story of Cardinal Gibbons' years at St. Charles may very well serve as the background for Cardinal O'Connell's experiences there. Here young William developed the desire for study and a thoroughgoing awakening of appreciation for the value of knowledge. Instruction was rather stiff and mechanical but was thorough. The teachers were the French Sulpicians with a long teaching tradition to guide them. There was no elective system and the boys studied hard for the spirit of application was in the air.

One thing the future cardinal missed very much, the opportunity to express himself in music. The piano at home had been a favorite resource. There was no such thing as a piano at St. Charles but one day young O'Connell found a wheezy old melodeon in the cellar and sat down to play some of his favorite music. He still has a taste and a love for music that represents his best resource in the midst of a busy life. Some of his compositions represent real contributions to hymnody. He forgot all about the passage of time as he played on and the bell rang for study hall without his taking any note of it. Suddenly he realized that some one was near him. He turned to find that it was Père Denis, the college president. The young musician was sure that he was in for some severe punishment for a violation of the rules, but the president said very kindly, "So you play! I was in the chapel and I heard the sounds from here below. I had quite forgotten the little melodeon. I came down wondering, to find you rapt in the music. The bell rang for studies but I decided not to disturb you. You love music. Well, that too is a gift of the good God. We must have the derelict repaired and then you shall come whenever you feel in the mood and no one shall disturb you, not even I."

Almost needless to say Père Denis became the young student's hero. He was also for many others of the students. His personality permeated the whole college. His Eminence still speaks of him to-day as the kindliest of men, and recalling his many acts of kindness says "He was a saint." It is extremely interesting to realize how much the spirit of an institution like this may be impersonated for many of the students at least in a single one of the professors. Père Denis deeply influenced not only the mind but the heart and soul of the future cardinal.

Application to study was at St. Charles the striking characteristic of student life. Most of them had come from families of the poorer class, they were deeply intent on taking advantage of every possible opportunity to secure an education and most of them had firmly decided that they wanted to be priests and the stirrings of their vocation represented constantly renewed incentives to go on with their work. During his first year at the college, young William O'Connell had devoted himself very ardently to his studies. The climate at St. Charles was not so bracing as that of northern Massachusetts and after a while the young student felt the effect of it. At the end of the year he was pretty well fagged out but the vacation seemed to renew all his health and strength. He went back in September to devote himself ardently to his studies, and as a result suffered from a breakdown which necessitated his giving up his studies for a time. Dear Père Denis advised him to go home and recuperate.

It did not take long for home cooking and the open air life to restore him to health but now instead of returning to St. Charles he resolved to enter Boston College. He devoted himself to his studies at home and hoped that he would be able to enter what was known as "poetry" class or what is now called Sophomore, at the college. When he applied at the college Father Fulton, the rector, gave him an examination and after nearly an hour without telling him the result of the examination took him round through the long corridor and halted

before a door over which was the sign "Poetry."
As they entered the room Father Fulton said to
Father Boursaud, the professor, "I have come to
bring you a new student." Young O'Connell had
made the class. What was more, he had the pleasure of hearing Father Fulton say, to his fellow
students, "If you don't work hard the new man will
take all the honors." Father Fulton who was afterwards Provincial of the Jesuits and visitor to several of the provinces in Europe was himself of
deep literary bent especially interested in poetry but
best known for his knowledge of men.

Cardinal O'Connell looks back now and is quite
ready to say that the happiest years of his life were
the three that he spent at his studies in Boston College. They were not easy years however. Owing
to family conditions William continued to live in
Lowell coming to Boston on the seven o'clock train
each morning. That meant rising at six or earlier,
for he had to have breakfast and preparations had
to be made for the day at school. A number of
students came in on that train, others from Boston
College, but some also who were in attendance at
the Massachusetts Institute of Technology or at
Harvard College as it was then known. They made
a happy, hearty group as a rule, thoroughly enjoy-
ing themselves, but the more studious of them among

whom was very often young O'Connell devoted themselves to the study of the day's lessons.

Boston College was then situated down on St. James Street where the high school still continues to have its classes though the college proper has moved out to University Heights, Chestnut Hill. It was the future cardinal's habit to walk every morning from the North Station to the college though the distance was fully two miles. In the bitter cold of some of the winter mornings that walk must have required a good deal of self-control to take. He was young and vigorous however, he had fully recovered from his breakdown and he thoroughly enjoyed the experience even on the coldest of days, while in the spring and fall the walk across the Common was an ideal preparation for a day's work in class.

He succeeded admirably in his studies and gave great satisfaction to his teachers. He devoted himself so assiduously to his work that his good mother began to fear lest he might injure his health once more. When she found him at study even after midnight, as she did from time to time, her mother heart would yearn to him and she insisted, "You must stop now and go to sleep. Your eyes are more important than your books." No one was prouder however of his success in his classes and she made it very clear to him that his devotion to his studies was one of her greatest consolations in life. When at the end of three years, at twenty-one, he graduated from Boston College he received the highest honors of the graduating class. The Governor of Massachusetts pinned three medals on him with the remark that he would need more room for medals if he continued to take prizes. When commencement was over his mother came to him and said "God bless you, child, you must be happy," and the cardinal has often said since that that was just like her. There was not a word about herself or her own happiness, always her children came first.

Now the question of his vocation to the priesthood came up for final determination and though the future cardinal still felt his unworthiness Archbishop Williams' words over the dead body of the youthful rector of the Boston Cathedral, Father Smith, who was also a Lowell boy, touched him deeply. The archbishop had said after words of the highest praise for the departed priest who had made himself beloved by all those who know him, "May God send this Church and this diocese more priests like him." These words brought the determination to young William O'Connell's heart that he would be a priest and he returned to Lowell and told his mother of his decision. There was to be no delay. He explained to her that he would ask the archbishop for adoption as one of the seminarians of the diocese on the very next day. "Thank God it is settled," is all that his mother replied.

Archbishop Williams received his application very graciously and recalled that the applicant had received the highest honors of the graduating class of Boston College that year. Because of this, the archbishop offered him his choice of a seminary for his theological studies. When young O'Connell hesitated over the choice, His Grace said, "Would you like to study in Rome?" There was nothing that the young student could wish for beyond that, and so it was settled that he should go to Rome. On his voyage over he landed in Ireland, visited the pretty Irish village where his mother and the older children had been born, and, after seeing London, and Paris in a hurried trip across the Continent, he reached Rome in the early morning and went straight to the American College. Here he had the opportunity of contact with some of the great minds of the Church. His professor in liturgy was a Greek archbishop, his professor of theology an Italian from Perugia, one of the most distinguished scholars of his day, while he was surrounded by men who were as varied in nationality and in speech as the crowd on the first Pentecost. There were

Greeks and Armenians, Arabs and Syrians, Africans and Asiatics, men of every race from every clime, all gathered hearing the same doctrine and learning the same lesson. The members of the different colleges sat in groups so that the different uniforms made a very striking picture.

Rome itself proved to be a great library for him, and he learned to love every stone of it, ancient and medieval, Renaissance and modern, as it was. It is easy to understand the broadening influence that some five years of study in Rome would mean for a mind acutely ready to receive impressions. After some four years of study, he was ordained to the priesthood June 8, 1884, by Cardinal Monaco in St. John Lateran. Toward the end of his course, young O'Connell's health had failed so that he had not been able to take the final examinations for the doctorate, and on the doctor's orders spent that summer vacation in the little fishing village of Anzio. He recuperated rather satisfactorily, though not completely, and returned to Rome to face the final year of work at the college. In addition to his studies he had been appointed first prefect of the college. In December, after two months of work, he was again in the doctor's care, and it seemed better for him not to pass another winter in Rome. He had to give up in sadness of heart his remaining work at college, and this meant the loss of his degree, for he could not remain for the examination.

His first assignment as a priest was as assistant at St. Joseph's Church in Medford, Mass. His first sermon attracted the old pastor's attention, who assured him that he had in him the makings of a good preacher. The young priest was particularly delighted with his work in the Sunday school. Children have always had a special appeal to him, and they gather round him in a way that shows very clearly that they appreciate his interest in them, for no one recognizes so soon as a child the fact that he is loved. This love for children has continued even down to the present day. Once in recent years, while on a visit to down-town Boston, the cardinal returned to his parked automobile to find a ragged, rather dirty little newsboy looking at it wistfully. "Gee, that's a fine auto," the boy said; "you bet I'd like to take a ride in an auto like that just once." "All right," His Eminence said cordially, "jump in." But the boy shook his head and pointed to his many unsold papers and made it clear that work must come before pleasure. His Eminence bought all the papers, insisted on the little fellow getting into the automobile and took him for a long ride, which was thoroughly enjoyed by both of them.

His pastor at Medford, Father Donnelly, having

died, Father O'Connell was appointed the curate of
St. Joseph's, one of the busiest of the Boston parishes.   This was in a tenement district with many
hospitals and jails, and there were many appeals for
aid, physical as well as spiritual, by night and day.
His first sick call at two o'clock in the morning was
to the Massachusetts General Hospital to a poor
woman burnt almost to a cinder, yet still alive and
needing if any one ever did the consolations of
religion.   At St. Joseph's the future cardinal was
thrown into contact with all the elements of Boston
city life and particularly those who needed his ministrations.   There were no less than eight hospitals in
the borders of the parish, a call from them might
come at any time, and then, besides, there were the
tenement houses from which night calls particularly
were not infrequent.   He had to be on duty practically twenty-four hours of the day.   He himself
has often said since that this gave him his opportunity to learn what it is to be a "working man."

Several years passed without a vacation, and then
he went to Chicago to attend the World's Fair.
After a single day there, he felt an unaccountable
restlessness and nostalgia.   He had never been homesick before, now something seemed to draw him to
his home.   He had meant to pass a week or more in
Chicago, instead he took a train East and then

thought he might stop in New York for a few days, but a vague uneasiness compelled him to push on to Lowell without delay. He found his mother dying; his sister said that they had vainly tried to reach him by telegraph in Chicago, and that they had given up hope of his reaching his mother before her death. As he walked into his mother's room, she stretched out her hand to him and whispered, "Thank God you came," and within half an hour she was dead. Just what the experience meant psychologically or spiritually the cardinal finds it difficult to say, but it gave him the precious happiness of bidding his mother a final adieu, and he would scarcely have forgiven himself if his one vacation for years had deprived him of that consolation for him and for her.

Meantime the Catholic Summer School had been founded, and after its preliminary meetings at New London, had been transferred to Plattsburg, N. Y., and Father O'Connell was asked to give a series of lectures there. These lectures proved very interesting to the select intellectual audiences of the early days at the Summer School and made it very clear to Catholics from all over the country that here was a new intellectual light that had come into the life of America. On the completion of the series the speaker was waited upon by a committee from the

Board of Trustees of the Summer School with the request that the lectures be put into permanent form. This proved to be his first published work, but has been followed by many others, until now there are some eight volumes* to the credit of His Eminence, all of them done in the midst of the very busy work demanded of him in the various positions that he has held.

In the early winter of the year after his Summer-School lectures, 1895, there came a cablegram from Rome, which contained the very brief announcement that Father O'Connell had been appointed to the rectorship of the American College at Rome. He had not had the slightest hint up to this time that he was even being considered for the position. It was not an easy one. The very existence of the college seemed even to be threatened for a while. Cardinal O'Connell has, however, never asked for an office by word or deed—and he has never refused to accept one when it was offered to him, no matter what burden it brought with it.

A few weeks later Father O'Connell was in active charge as the rector of the American College. It had not changed from what it had been when he

* The cardinal's printed works consist of *Sermons and Addresses,* in seven volumes, and *The Life of Christ* by Cardinal DeLai, translated by him. The discourses contained in the *Sermons and Addresses* are not homiletic essays but stirring addresses on the particular needs of the time.

left it as a student a dozen years before. At his
first interview with Pope Leo XIII the Pope said
to him, "I am deeply concerned for the success of
the American College, and I know that you will give
it all your attention. You are young and strong, I
see. That is well, for you will need all of your
strength. You are rather young for the position"—
this with a pleasant smile—"but old enough if you
follow good advice." The Pope assured him that
while there was a great task before him for one so
young, with God's help he would surely do it well.
This was encouragement indeed.

The new rector of the American College found
the institution almost bankrupt. Fortunately he was
able to secure sources of support for it and gradually
to restore it to its place as a worthy representative
of the great American republic in Rome. The college was sadly in need of a summer home, and
Father O'Connell was able to secure the funds to
purchase this, obtaining for the purpose a beautiful
old palace, splendidly appointed, with a charming
private chapel, surrounded by sixty acres of wooded
park. The most valuable endorsement of his rectorship, however, came in the increase from year to
year of the number of students at the college.

It was not surprising then that at the end of some
two years Father O'Connell was summoned to the

Vatican one day, and as he knelt to receive the Pope's blessing he had the happiness of hearing the Pope say, "We are very content with your work. It is excellent, excellent indeed, and now it is time to give you a testimony of our approval. I name you one of the prelates of the household of the pope. You are now *Monsignore O'Connell, prelato domestico di sua santità,*" Father O'Connell was not yet forty, and the beginning of his ecclesiastical honors had come to him.

His success at the American College continued, the college itself prospered, the number of students doubled, until it was no wonder that a prominent member of the College of Cardinals in Rome said to the rector one day, "We shall always consider you the second founder of the American College." After the first two years, there was opportunity to relax, and the young monsignor, with the special honors of the Holy Father still fresh upon him, found that the social life of Rome now opened its doors to him, and that there were many distinguished members of the Italian nobility as well as other dwellers in Rome who were glad to honor the rector of so successful an institution as the American College had now become.

The college continued to be, however, his constant solicitude, but one that, instead of being a source of worry, was a delight to his heart. He has himself said that he probably never performed more congenial work than as the rector of the American College. Early in his career there he had gathered the students about him and declared, "I will never consent to be merely a policeman over you." His conferences twice a week to the boys came to be events that were looked forward to. The college under his guidance came to be as successful in scholarship and in discipline as it was in administration and finance.

He had been just six years at the American College when in April, 1901, he received a brief message from Cardinal Ledochowski, notifying him of his appointment as Bishop of Portland, Maine. This appointment, so well deserved in recognition of his fine work for the American College, came to him quite unexpectedly. He was consecrated by Cardinal Satolli in the beautiful Corsini Chapel, and the co-consecrators were Monsignor Merry del Val and Monsignor Stonor. It was at this consecration that the social prominence which had accrued to the rector of the American College was very clearly demonstrated, for the solemn ceremony was witnessed by a very large representation of the great Roman families of the nobility who had been so friendly and hospitable during his stay in Rome, but also by the American ambassador and by many members of the American colony in Rome.

Bishop O'Connell was to remain in Portland a scant five years, but during that time he made many friends, above all among non-Catholics, though the religious atmosphere of Maine is inclined to be rather bigoted. The governor of the state said to him one day, shortly after he came to Portland, "Bishop O'Connell, I think this state owes you an official reception. I have talked the matter over with some friends, and they agree with me, and I want to give you that official welcome." "But I didn't know," replied the bishop, "that any representative of any church is ever officially received by the state." "That's very true," the governor replied promptly, "they never are, but I want to make an exception in your case." So a few days later Bishop O'Connell, in his robes for an official ceremony, mounted the steps of the State House in Portland, was received by members of the governor's staff, who escorted him to the executive chambers, where the governor awaited him, and bade him an official welcome in the name of the state of Maine. It was all most formal, but it has been said that it was all most unprecedented. Probably a similar event had never before occurred in this country, certainly not in that particular state.

During his third year in Portland, there came to Bishop O'Connell a cable from the papal Secretary of State at Rome, announcing that he had been appointed special papal ambassador to the Emperor of Japan. As the representative of the Holy See, he was directed to go immediately to Japan and there to enter into negotiations with the Emperor to arrange for the protection of all Catholic missionaries in Japan. No one knew better than he how serious this mission was and how difficult its successful accomplishment might be. This was shortly after the end of the Russo-Japanese War, and the Japanese people, especially those in the cities, were passing through one of the periodic outbursts of feeling against foreigners. Some missionaries had been captured, and some of them put to death, and others expelled from the country. In all the western countries there was a feeling of uneasiness as to the situation in the Far East. It seemed as though it would be almost impossible to conclude such a mission satisfactorily.

Fortunately, while Bishop O'Connell was on the way to Japan, the anti-foreign party in that country was swept out of power and a more liberal cabinet took its place. His mission, therefore, proved preeminently successful. Bishop O'Connell was received most cordially, and during the months of negotiations that followed he was frequently received by the Emperor and by other members of the imperial family. Every request which as papal ambassador he made to the Japanese government was granted in full. Besides he was cordially honored in a personal way, and the Grand Cordon of the Sacred Treasure was conferred on him. His stay in Japan was capped by an elaborate official function given in Bishop O'Connell's honor, at which the Prime Minister of Japan arose and proposed a toast to His Holiness the Pope. This was followed by a personal farewell address to the papal ambassador, in which the highest appreciation of his conduct at the embassy was expressed. The popular farewell expressed by an escort through the streets and by a large assemblage of people from every walk of life was almost unprecedented in the history of the country.

Bishop O'Connell proceeded to Rome to make a formal report of the results of his embassy to the pope. He reached there in January, 1906. Immediately after the audiences at the Vatican he planned to return to Portland, feeling that his diocese needed his attention. On the day before his departure from Rome he received word of his appointment as Coadjutor Archbishop of Boston. He was received very warmly by Archbishop Williams, who had always had him specially in his heart since the day he suggested his going as a seminarian to Rome. His coadjutor was particularly welcome because the archbishop's life was ebbing. Before the end of the year Archbishop Williams died, leaving the duties and honors of the archbishopric of Boston on Archbishop O'Connell's shoulders.

During Archbishop Williams' declining years a great many problems had developed in the archdiocese of Boston of which the elderly archbishop had put off the solution. All these now came to Archbishop O'Connell for disposal. Parishes had become very large and unwieldy, divisions of parishes had not been made, many phases of Catholicity had been allowed to sink into desuetude, and a firm hand guided by a head of strong administrative ability was needed. The present condition of the archdiocese of Boston as told in the second portion of this sketch furnishes the best possible demonstration of how much he accomplished.

Some of Cardinal O'Connell's expressions reveal the man very thoroughly. He declared once, "I have known four popes, three of them intimately, and to my mind the greatest of them all was Pope Pius X." He added, "I consider Pope Pius X the greatest chiefly because of the stand which he took toward all nations as regards diplomatic relations

with the Holy See. He insisted that the primary
duty of the pope was a spiritual one, and under his
leadership the Church wrested itself free from
diplomacy." Cardinal O'Connell's advice to young
men was to have faith in God first, last and all the
time, and with it what is called, and so well called,
a saving sense of humor. The cardinal finds his
relaxation at times in the reading of novels, and
especially those of an exciting character. Mystery
stories of various kinds that are ingeniously told
serve to distract him from the affairs of his archdiocese when these might otherwise weigh heavily
on him. He is a great reader and every week goes
over a dozen or more books, skimming some, dip-
ping lightly into others, but devoting no little time
to not a few of them. He has a habit, acquired
while he was abroad, of reading certain of the Con-
tinental newspapers, and as a man who has made
a success in three continents and who has a background of broad interest in world affairs that makes
his judgment with regard to current events of striking value, he feels that he must keep in direct touch
with world affairs.

What has been accomplished in the archdiocese
of Boston during the present archiepiscopate is very
well revealed by the increase in the number of institutions for those who are not able to care for

themselves, which have been erected and enlarged, and the increase in the number of charitable purposes that has come. In the volume entitled *A Brief Historical Review of the Archdiocese of Boston, 1907-1923* (Boston, 1924), all this is summed up succinctly as follows:—

"1st—there are now 53 such institutions in the Diocese as against 23 in 1907;

"2nd—this represents an increase of about 150 per cent;

"3rd—while the 23 in 1907 served 6 distinct charitable purposes, those of 1923 serve 14;

"4th—of the 23 institutions in existence in 1907, 19, or 90 per cent, of them have been supplanted by entirely new structures or enlarged very considerably to meet present-day requirements;

"5th—the approximate valuation of diocesan charitable institutions in 1907 was $3,500,000 as against a valuation to-day of about $7,500,000."

The building up of the spirit has gone hand in hand with the construction of church property. The chapter called "A Spiritual Survey" in the historical review just cited is illuminating in this regard. In our time, when the complaint everywhere is of the falling off of Church membership and the lack of attendance at services, it is indeed interesting to learn that there is an average attendance of 800,000

men, women and children at Mass on each Sunday
of the year in the Boston archdiocese. The records
of the various parishes show that there is an increase during the past twenty years of nearly 250,-
000 in the Catholic population of the archdiocese.
Not long after the decree of Pope Piux X on Daily
Communion, His Eminence of Boston addressed to
the priests and laity of his diocese a striking letter
during the Lenten season on this salutary practice.
The result has been that in the course of the past ten
years daily Communions have mounted in number
to three million in the year, First Friday and feast-
day Communions have reached four million, and
the number of Communions on Sunday has reached
the splendid figure of ten millions.

What is known as the Night Workers' Mass has
had the special solicitude of the cardinal archbishop. This Mass was inaugurated twenty-one
years ago on the appeal of a group of printers and
other newspaper employees. At the first Mass there
were seventy-five present. In a few months, the number doubled. It is easy to understand what a great
convenience this was for these working people.
After hearing Mass they could go home and rest
perfectly quiet until midday on Sunday, making it
a real day of rest and without any anxiety about
having to get up for attendance at Mass at ten or

eleven. In 1914, through the interest of the cardinal archbishop, this Mass, celebrated at three-thirty, was transferred to St. James Church in the south end, where on Sundays and holidays of obligation nearly one thousand men and women, representing all classes of night workers in Boston, find a convenient opportunity to hear Mass and receive Holy Communion.

Church societies have claimed the special attention of the cardinal, for he realized the necessity for solidarity of men and women as a means of encouragement to one another for the right performance of their Christian duty. Example is ever so much better than precept, and social incentive is the most important element for conduct in life. His Eminence has frequently urged the pastors of his diocese to develop on broader lines the two religious societies of the Church, the Holy Name Society for the men and the Sodality for the women.

In New England it would, of course, be expected that education would be the outstanding factor in the diocesan work, and such it has proved to be, and the increase in Catholic educational facilities and the way they have been taken advantage of during the period of Cardinal O'Connell's occupation of the position of archbishop has been very wonderful. There has been really an immense advance, almost amounting to doubling the numbers of the pupils, in the not quite twenty years that have elapsed during the present archbishopric. What is even more significant is the fact that there has been at the same time a steady upward progress in the development of high-school and college work. Figures in this matter are almost startling in their evidence of increased interest and growth. In 1908 there were 170 pupils enrolled in colleges, and in 1924 there were 1,149 on the rolls. There has been a very great increase also in the percentage of enrollment in both high schools and colleges in proportion to the number of pupils in the elementary schools. Fifteen years ago only a little more than 3 per cent of the elementary school pupils continued their studies into high school, and less than four-hundredths of 1 per cent entered college. Now nearly 8 ½ per cent of the common school pupils take high-school work, and nearly 1 ½ per cent of the elementary school pupils go to college.

Very probably the most interesting phase for the modern time of the development of the life of the spirit in the Boston archdiocese is to be found in the revivification of the old guilds which meant so much in the medieval Church. The most significant of the Boston guilds is the Guild of St. Luke, in whose ranks are gathered the Catholic physicians of Boston and its neighborhood. This was originally organized some ten years ago and now includes several hundred Boston physicians, with a spiritual director, Right Reverend Monsignor Splaine, appointed by the cardinal. The cardinal himself acts as honorary president and has always been interested in the activities of the guild. Regular meetings are held, at which important medical topics that have a bearing on religion are discussed and the ethical principles of medical practice brought out. As a result of their association, Catholic physicians of Boston are brought closely together, and they constitute an important conservative element in the medical profession. The tendency in medicine is to be run away with by novel notions of various kinds, and a balance wheel of this nature is extremely important. In the past such practices as craniotomy on living children had been allowed to become serious abuses when, as became clear later, there was no need for them, and when they represented grave danger to mother as well as the inevitable death of the child.

One of the self-imposed burdens of the Guild of St. Luke is very interesting because it represents the sort of duty towards others' and especially the benighted poor, that some people find rather difficult to understand. While Professor Thomas Dwight, the well-known professor of anatomy at Harvard, was in charge of the dissecting room at the university, he made it a point to have Masses said for the souls of the persons whose bodies were brought to the dissecting room. They had died absolutely friendless, otherwise their bodies would not, under the anatomical law, have come into the possession of the anatomical department. Since Professor Dwight's death, the Guild of St. Luke has taken over this charitable obligation, and Masses are said every year for the persons whose bodies find their way for dissecting purposes to the various medical schools in the district.

There are more strictly professional interests, however, that form part of the annual program of the guild. Public clinics are held twice a year at St. Elizabeth's and Carney Hospitals, and they bring the members together for the discussion of medical and surgical questions. These occasions accomplish much to make their relations to one another friendly and intimate. Some of the most prominent members of the profession in and around Boston have been willing to take on themselves the added burden of holding official positions in the guild for the sake of the ethical influence it represented. The late Dr. John Bottomley, one of the most distinguished of New England surgeons, was deeply interested in the guild and made many sacrifices in the display of that interest.

The next most interesting of these guilds is the Guild of St. Appollonia which comprises the Catholic dentists of Boston under the ægis of the patron saint of dentistry, St. Appollonia. The guild was organized five years ago and is the only one of its kind in the country. Since its formation the guild in coöperation with the Forsyth Dental Infirmary has accomplished the great good work of caring for the dental needs of nearly 50,000 children in the parochial schools of greater Boston. Indeed the care of these parochial-school children was really the primary purpose in establishing the guild. In the public schools arrangements were made so that the children's teeth are cared for and something of the same kind was needed for the Catholic parochial schools. Unfortunate habits of eating and especially the elimination to a great extent of the tougher materials from the diet and the eating of "slops" has done much to make children's teeth ever so much less healthy than they used to be and has brought about the occurrence of caries even in the earlier years so that the milk teeth have to be cared for scientifically so as not to permit injury to the permanent teeth as they erupt.

In five years the guild has grown to such an extent that it now includes over two hundred members most of whom have taken some part in the special work of caring for the school children's teeth. It was hoped that this organization of the dentists into a guild in Boston would provide an example that would be followed in other cities and already there are signs that the splendid success of the Boston guild is going to be productive of corresponding organizations in other parts of the country. In the meantime they have met with every encouragement from Cardinal O'Connell who has congratulated them very heartily. He has assured them that he knows that if they work together "out of this guild of a couple of hundred men will come a great work. You can inaugurate a work that will spread through every Christian country in the world." As one who has been present at some of their functions to take a part however small in their discussions, the work of this guild appeals as a rejuvenescence in the best sense of the word of some of the old medieval guild work which meant so much for making life happier not only for those for whom work was done but above all for those who did work for others in the medieval period, which at last we are coming to understand.

It is not however only among the men that these guilds with all their traditional influence for good as exemplified in the medieval period have been organized. In connection with the Cenacle as it is called, that is the religious congregation of nuns whose principal object is the affording of an opportunity for girls and women to make retreats, a series of guilds have been organized among the women engaged in various occupations in the archdiocese. The chief retreat house of this congregation, called the Cenacle in honor of the Upper Room in which the Apostles met with the Master for his Last Supper, was established in Brighton by His Eminence, Cardinal O'Connell, on October 10, 1910. Almost immediately after the foundation of the Cenacle in the early part of 1911, three guilds for women were organized. These were St. Anne's Association for married women, the Association of the Cenacle for business women, and the Association of St. Regis for teachers. Through these guilds various groups of women and girls were brought to the convent every month to spend a day in prayer and recollection, to assist at a conference given by one of the clergy, and in this way to be prepared to fulfill the paramount regulations of the guild which concerns the making of an annual retreat. The essence of religion is within us and does not consist in external observances nor in formal words of petition or even thanksgiving, but in such meditation of the mind and heart and soul as lets the mystery of things speak to us.

In the following year, 1912, two other guilds were established and began corresponding good work. The first of these was the Guild of St. Genesius for stenographers and those occupied with secretarial work. One of the significant features of these guilds is the choice of a patron for them and St. Genesius (whose Acts were probably written by St. Paulinus of Nola) was a soldier noted for his proficiency in writing, who became the secretary to the magistrate of Arles. In this position the decree of persecution against the Christians in the time of the Emperor Maximianus at the beginning of the fourth century passed through his hands and so outraged his sense of justice that he proclaimed himself a Christian and as a martyr was baptized in his own blood. His veneration is one of the oldest traditions in the Church for he is found in an ancient martyrology ascribed to St. Jerome. It is easy to understand that the inspiration of association under such a patron would mean very much for a sense of courageous facing of difficulties and especially for the refusal to have any part in any underhand public dishonesty, a quality needed in our day.

The second of these guilds of 1912 was the Guild of St. Zita who is the Church's model and heavenly patroness of domestic service. The organization of the guild represents one of the few attempts if not the only one made in this country to give a definite standing to those engaged in domestic service and produce in them the feeling that theirs is a vocation in life that one may be proud of and content in. In imitation of their patroness, St. Zita, they occupy themselves in domestic affairs since these represent such care for the necessities of the bodies of men and women as makes it possible for them to be occupied with higher things. The labor of the daughters of St. Zita though merely manual may thus help to increase the intellectual or artistic heritage of the generation, because it lifts the burden of ordinary everyday affairs from the shoulders of those who would otherwise find it difficult to secure the time for higher things.

Still the spirit of the Cenacle proved inspiring and in 1914 the Guild of St. Agnes for high-school girls was organized anticipating some of the difficulties that were coming with the modern flapper and introducing an appropriate feeling of personal responsibility for example to others to these young women of the transition period. In 1919 the Guild of St. Imelda for factory girls was organized and the Guild of the Presentation of the Blessed Virgin for telephone operators. At the beginning of the work the various activities were conducted under difficulties because of limited accommodations, but in spite of this handicap much was accomplished and in May, 1912, under the inspiration and encouragement of the cardinal, a new building was opened. During the course of the rest of that year eight retreats were given with more than 200 in attendance and nearly 1,500 took part in the Day of Recollection. Every year since, the attendance has continued to mount. The number nearly doubled in 1913. In 1920 altogether twenty retreats were given with nearly 1,000 retreatants and well above 6,000 took part in the Day of Recollection. Besides 120 private retreats were conducted. The numbers have constantly grown. In 1921 there were nearly 12,000 who took part in the Day of Recollection. During the course of this work in the Boston archdiocese some 20,000 women have made the annual retreat of three days and over 100,000 have attended the monthly Day of Recollection.

Almost needless to say this represents that personal devotion and occupation with religious ideas and meditation on religious truths that lift people up above the sordid material world and give them thoughts that breathe and words that burn into their souls and that make life ever so much more worth living because it is lived on a higher plane.

What was thus accomplished for the women in 1910 had been anticipated by corresponding efforts made for the organization of a house of retreats for men under the care of the Passionists. In order to promote devotion to the sufferings of the Lord as a source of consolation in the trials and afflictions inevitable in life, His Eminence invited these fathers whose life is devoted to the idea of making Christ's sufferings better understood to establish a foundation in the archdiocese. At his suggestion the Nevins Estate was purchased on top of one of the hills in Brighton making a wonderfully convenient location and one at the same time retired and altogether suitable for retreats. The first chapel of the fathers was not unsuitably a stable which by ingenious and loving care had been transformed into a thing of beauty.

After the work had been in progress but four years the cardinal dedicated, May 14, 1911, the present handsome building where the first retreat was given on December 8th of that year. In the course of ten years the number of retreats had grown to three with an annual attendance of over a thousand men. During the same length of time nearly two thousand men made private retreats showing how close to the heart of humanity is this thought of withdrawal from the affairs of the practical busy life to get a chance to think out the meaning of things.

Altogether within a dozen of years well above 25,000 men of all kinds have made retreats here. There have been business men and bankers but also newspaper men, professors at colleges, manual laborers, railroad men, white collar clerks and artisans, often finding inspiration in the companionship of the retreats because of the many and varied interests which they represented. Retreats are not a time for hours of conversation but men become acquainted with each other and under such circumstances learn to appreciate each other's point of view until there is a real socializing of the men thus brought together that is very interesting and not one of the least of the good effects of the retreats. No very special effort has been made to produce this fine effect but it has simply been made known that those who wished might spend a week-end mainly devoted to prayer and meditation and yet with such relaxation of spirit as was of itself thoroughly recreating. Many a man has said that he got more benefit out of his week-end retreat than out of a couple of weeks of vacation. After all it is not doing nothing that rests men but finding diversion of mind and undoubtedly one of the reasons why a great many of the contemplative religious live such long lives is because they find real diversion and satisfaction of mind in their quiet efforts at intimate communication with the Powers whose ordered universe around us is such a mystery unless understood in terms of the Fatherhood of God and the brotherhood of man.

With the very definite organization of the spiritual side of archdiocesan work, it is not surprising to learn that the number of converts to the Church has gone on increasing until now well above a thousand are baptized every year. In order to make the coming into the Church of this large number of adults, many of them deeply intelligent, some of them at least thoroughly educated, all of them as a rule with the benefit of our American school education, properly impressive, the cardinal has organized the ceremony of confirmation for them each year in the cathedral. There is a special mission for non-Catholics given in the cathedral and at the end of this hundreds of men and women from all parts of the diocese are assembled and receive Confirmation from the cardinal archbishop himself. This is one of the functions that particularly delights his heart and from which he does not absent himself except by absolute necessity.

It has often been said that besides the apostolate of the pulpit the Church in our day needs the apostolate of the press and of the lecture platform. These have not been neglected in the archdiocese of Boston. In 1907 the Catholic Truth Guild was organized under the patronage of His Eminence and is entirely a laymen's movement in the interest of the diffusion of Catholic truth. The well-known Catholic Evidence Guild of England was organized a year later and the influence of the Boston organization seems to have been felt in that. The idea was to go out into the highways and the byways and make Catholic truth known. Street campaigning was not a familiar mode of procedure in Catholic work and there were some forebodings as to the results. The auto van built for the purpose however has not only gone around Massachusetts but has actually crossed the continent, traveling from city to city for some 13,000 miles, and not one untoward incident occurred to make priests or laymen feel that the open-air campaign was inopportune. During its seven years of activity about 100 meetings have been held each year and on the average 10,000 cloth-bound Catholic books and a total of 50,000 pamphlets have been sold annually.

A second form of lay activity in Boston with the purpose of helping to disseminate truth with regard to the Catholic Church is the Common Cause Forum. Franklin Union Hall, in which it holds its meetings has a seating capacity of 1,200 and it is often filled to capacity and sometimes it is impossible for many of those who have come even from a distance to get in. A Catholic lecturer addresses the audience for an hour and then free discussion is allowed with the lecturer closing the discussion. The Common Cause Forum opens its doors freely to all comers but it is the only large forum in Boston where free discussion is permitted. There is a chaplain who presides at the meetings but though there is a time limit on those who address the meetings apart from the speaker of the evening, there is the completest freedom of expression. This seems to many people all the more surprising because they are not accustomed to associate the idea of such liberty of spirit and of speech with the Catholic Church and its activities. They forget that the Church is the most logical institution in the world and that while reason and faith are quite different mental attributes, Catholics are taught to know the reasons for the faith that is in them and any educated Catholic has a better conviction as to the meaning of life and the world around us, a better *Weltanschaung* than any one who has not received the training afforded by Church teaching.

Very probably the most interesting phase of Catholic life in Boston is the number of young men and young women who have sacrificed their worldly careers whole-heartedly to take up the special service of the Church. During the past fifteen years, in this twentieth century when life seems so vivid and when otherworldliness seems to many people so distant, over 5,000 young men and women have given themselves to the Church. The number is increasing in recent years and not diminishing though almost needless to say the opposite experience is that which forms the subject of complaint in most churches. During the past ten years more than twice as many seminarians have been ordained priests at the Boston Seminary as during the preceding ten years. Besides large numbers of young men from the Boston archdiocese have entered the religious orders particularly the Augustinians, the Jesuits, the Oblates, the Passionists, the Redemptorists and the Vincentians. The city of Boston itself is particularly luxuriant in vocations to the priesthood both secular and religious. It is said that over 700 natives of Boston are ordained every year to the priesthood.

The archdiocese of Boston has become famous throughout the world for its contributions to the support of missionaries and especially for its collections for the Society for the Propagation of the Faith. It is no wonder that Cardinal Van Rossum, Prefect of the Sacred Congregation of Propaganda, who is at the head of all mission activities throughout the world, has more than once expressed his appreciation of the cordial relations which exist between the Boston archdiocese and Propaganda and has pointed to Boston as a model diocese in the field of mission aid. There are branches of the Society for the Propagation of the Faith in every parish. How thoroughly alive to mission needs these are will be best understood from the fact that over $100,000 is contributed every year from about 150 branches, an average of over $700 from each one. There has been a constant increase in the funds and the leading parish each year has made an ever higher contribution. In 1922, St. Eulalia's in South Boston gave over $12,500 but in 1923 St. Cecelia's of Boston gave $18,500 and already it is clear that the banner parish will give over $20,000 a year.

New England has always been interested in the colored man and his uplift, but it has remained for the Catholic archdiocese of Boston to be the leader in the provision of missionary material for the conversion of the negroes to the Catholic Church. In a letter from the superior of the Josephites, the Very Reverend Louis Pastorelli, who was himself from Boston, and Boston's first member of the Society of the Josephites, whose work is exclusively as missionaries among the colored folk at the South, he states that the members of the Society from Boston number seven priests, nine seminarians, and forty-five collegians. The Society has in all thirty-one seminarists, and one hundred and three collegians. This means that Boston has supplied almost one-third of the seminarians and nearly half of the younger men in colleges who are preparing for the work of the colored missions. Among the sister-hoods devoted to the Indians and negroes Boston is well represented and the cardinal encourages in every way the spirit of self-sacrifice which tempts men and women to give themselves to the great work of missions among the colored races in our own country.

In the foreign mission field Boston has been especially preëminent. Until the coming of its present archbishop, Boston had but one missionary in the foreign field. He was in India. Now there are missionaries from Boston in China, India, Indo-China, Africa, Oceania and the Philippines. They comprise Jesuits, Franciscans, Passionists, Vincentians, Marists, and Maryknollers.

The greatest contribution to the foreign mission field was the Very Reverend James A. Walsh, founder and superior of the Catholic Foreign Mission Society of America and of the Missionary Sisters of St. Dominic, whose great work at Maryknoll (Ossining, N. Y.) is one of the special triumphs of the Church in America. Father Walsh was the Boston diocesan director of the Society for the Propagation of the Faith (1903-1911) when he conceived the splendid purpose of founding an American Catholic foreign mission society through which we would supply not only funds but men and women from among Americans for the mission field. That work has been a wonderful success. Father Walsh wrote recently that more than one-eighth of the students in the seminary, one-seventh of the boys in the preparatory school, and more than one-third of the sisters vowed to the missions are from the archdiocese of Boston.

Another very interesting development in the mission field undertaken during the present cardinal archbishop's episcopate was the establishment of the Association of the Holy Child. A dozen years ago this work was almost unknown. Its purpose is to get boys and girls under the banner of the Christ Child interested in the question of saving children, both body and soul, on the distant missions. In 1914 altogether only about a thousand boys and girls were enrolled in it. A single appeal to the parish priests and the sisters effected within a year the introduction of the Association to very nearly one hundred schools instead of the five to which it was limited before, and the enrollment jumped to nearly 40,000. Now there is an enrollment of over 150,000 girls and boys, and the pennies of the children have mounted up from year to year until where ten years ago there was less than $2,500 a year for a great purpose, there is now some $30,000 available. The interest aroused in the hearts and minds of the children undoubtedly accomplishes even more than what their gifts mean for the youthful impressions are sure to be lasting and the habit of interest in missionary activities thus acquired will never die out.

The work of the Society for the Propagation of the Faith has developed even more strikingly than that of the Association of the Holy Child. In 1898 less than $1,500 was contributed. Last year the contribution amounted to over $600,000. Altogether over 700 missionaries and 232 dioceses and vicariates are being helped from Boston, and the offerings made during the twenty-five years which represent the first quarter of the twentieth century amount to over $5,000,000. Over 90 per cent of this has been collected and remitted since Cardinal O'Connell became Archbishop of Boston. The most recent reports show a contribution to missions of almost $1.00 per year from each Catholic child, as well as adult, in the diocese. Cardinal O'Connell has encouraged this work in every way, and he has insisted that there is nothing which means so much for the preservation and diffusion of the faith at home as a persevering interest in foreign missions. As he himself has said, "Let us never forget this, to keep the faith ourselves we must propagate it."

Boston's school system has not only been extended very wonderfully under the present cardinal archbishop, but there has also been an intensive advance in school work more than corresponding to the growth of the school. In 1914 the archbishop appointed a Board of Community Supervisors of Schools. Each community teaching two thousand children in the schools of the archdiocese was given a representative on this board which consisted of twelve members representing ten religious communities. The schools conducted by their respective communities are visited at regular intervals, local school problems are studied, and assistance and guidance are given to the teacher in the classroom. The result has been the development of an excellent spirit of coöperation and a coördination of effort with striking results. In 1915 a special supervisor for the study of music was appointed by the archbishop, for whom music is the prince of arts, and the consequence has been that parochial-school pupils receive a very satisfactory training in the theory and practice of music during their early and impressionable years.

In 1915 a beginning was made to unify the work in the elementary grades of the parochial schools of the archdiocese. An outline of requirements was drawn up to be accomplished in each grade from the first to the eighth. After eight years of experience with this, suggestions were asked from supervisors and teachers for the improvement of the original outline. The curriculum in religion, English, arithmetic, history, civics, patriotism, geography, music, drawing, physical training and physiology and hygiene, has been elaborated in such a way as to provide the easiest method and at the same time the most thorough knowledge. Particular attention has been given to the proper teaching of American history, civics and patriotism to meet the duties and responsibilities which life in the United States places on every individual.

Over and over again Cardinal O'Connell's recognition of the really worth-while elements in the lives of members of the priesthood of his diocese especially in what concerns the influence that churchmen can have for humanity because of their ecclesiastical condition, has been expressed so straightforwardly as to leave no doubt as to his own feelings as to these values in life. He has picked out men who have lived quiet, simple but earnest, zealous lives to laud them as examples of what can and ought to be accomplished by priests who have the best interests of the Church at heart.

The most recent striking illustration of this is to be found in what he said of the late Very Reverend James T. O'Reilly, pastor of St. Mary's Church, Lawrence, Massachusetts, at the funeral of that veteran son of St. Augustine, forty years of whose priestly life was spent at St. Mary's and who had come to be looked upon by all the people of Lawrence no matter what Church or creed they belonged to, as the pastor of all of the people of the town. His influence was very widespread and was of the finest kind. It is such lives as this that make the Church stand out as veritably continuing the ministry of Christ in the bringing of peace to men of good will on earth.

Father O'Reilly had come to occupy almost national attention during the I. W. W. troubles some years ago in Lawrence when during the strike, anarchy raised its head and men carried banners through the streets with the legend, "No God, no master." It was then as on similar occasions before in times of industrial disturbance that the personal popularity of Father O'Reilly among the citizens of all classes and creeds proved one of the most efficient factors in the allaying of bitter feelings so that as the Governor of Massachusetts so well said, his personal influence did much to suppress lawlessness, disorder and anarchy.

In his funeral oration Cardinal O'Connell said, after having proclaimed Father O'Reilly's greatness of heart and soul, "One of the most difficult things in the whole world is to analyze the secret of greatness. The world is often mistaken in its estimate of a man because those of the world do not always see clearly. Father O'Reilly was undoubtedly a great character; when called upon to name the strong qualities of his character it is not difficult if one knows the fountain from whose source these qualities come. He had that rare combination of strength and gentleness that makes a great man. Many have one and lack the other. The strong are sometimes too strong and with the quality of gentleness often goes that of weakness. In him whom we honor to-day the qualities of greatness and strength supplemented one another."

While Cardinal O'Connell has thus deeply appreciated the labors of those whose long years of occupation in the archdiocese have given them a place of honor and reverence in the hearts of the faithful and his own efforts have been mainly directed to the flock entrusted to his care, he has not forgotten that there are others not of the fold who deserve his solicitude and for whom he bears a definite responsibility. As was true in Rome and in Portland, those not of the Faith who have been brought in contact with him have learned to admire him very much and to appreciate his personality and to reverence his ecclesiastical character. New England has gradually been transformed in the course of time until the proportion of Catholics in the population gives them a political prestige undreamed of in the older time. Some of the states actually have a considerable majority of Catholics in their population. It is well then that the representative New England cardinal, the head of the hierarchy, enjoys the respect and esteem of Catholics and non-Catholics alike and that he is in such honor in his own country.

DENNIS, CARDINAL DOUGHERTY

Fifth American Cardinal

Dennis Joseph Dougherty who on March 7,
1921, was created the fifth cardinal to be elevated
to that rank in the hierarchy in the United States,
was born August 16, 1865. His parents were then
living within the bounds of the present parish of
Girardville, Schuylkill County, Pennsylvania, though
at that time the parish of Girardville had not as yet
been erected, but formed part of St. Joseph's parish,
Ashland, in the same county. Cardinal Dougherty
is one of the small-town men who so often impress
themselves deeply upon their generation. Not long
after his birth his family moved into the town of
Ashland where he lived until he was nearly ten
years of age, when his parents returned to Girardville.

He received his education until the age of ten
years in the public schools of Ashland and until the
age of fifteen in those of Girardville. His parents
who were very faithful Catholics would surely have
sent him to the parochial school had there been

CARDINAL DOUGHERTY

one in the neighborhood. As it was they were ready
and willing to make sacrifices to afford him a Catholic college education just as soon as he was capable
of it and accordingly in September of his fifteenth
year, 1880, he entered the Jesuit College at St.
Mary's, Bleury Street, Montreal, Canada, where
he continued his studies for the next few years.
This gave him an excellent command of French as
well as a solid foundation in the classics. In September, 1882, he entered St. Charles Seminary,
Overbrook, Pennsylvania, just outside of Philadelphia, to complete his classical course and make his
preparatory studies of philosophy in preparation
for the priesthood. He spent the next three years
there as a student giving abundant evidence of excellent talents and solidity of character capable of
thorough training.

It is not surprising then that in September, 1885,
he was chosen by the Archbishop of Philadelphia
to enter the North American college at Rome.
This is the great Roman mother of bishops for the
United States and probably no better opportunity
for the obtaining of broad culture and an exquisite
classical background for education could be obtained
than is provided by the years of study in Rome.
The future cardinal spent the next five years taking the best possible advantage of the opportunities

for breadth and depth of education afforded by his environment. He displayed talents which showed very clearly that here was an exceptional man. He was ordained to the priesthood on May 31, 1890, by Cardinal Parocchi, in the Basilica of St. John Lateran, the mother church of Latin Christianity. A few weeks later his academic work of five years in Rome was crowned by the reception of the degree of Doctor of Divinity from the great Roman College of the Propaganda. This is a very enviable distinction which only the more talented and studious of the Roman students secure but which stamps a man as of high intellectual ability and thoroughgoing power of thought. Roman doctors from the Propaganda are as a rule men who in later life are the leaders among their fellows of the ecclesiastical world and usually they are chosen as the teachers in diocesan seminaries throughout the world and almost invariably are destined for places in the hierarchy in their later careers. Upon his return to Philadelphia as might almost inevitably have been anticipated under the circumstances young Father Dougherty—he was but twenty-five years of age—was appointed to a professorship on the staff of St. Charles Seminary, Overbrook, the diocesan seminary of Philadelphia. He took up his duties in September, 1890. Here he spent the next dozen years of his life in the quiet hard work of seminary professorship attracting attention by the thoroughness of his teaching, the absolute regularity of his life and by his devotion to duty and his spiritual mindedness. Here in the early years of the twentieth century his first advancement in the hierarchy came to him when he was appointed by Pope Leo XIII as Bishop of Nueva Segovia, Northern Luzon, in the Philippine Islands. In the course of his teaching at Overbrook he had become the professor of dogmatic theology there and had reached the culmination of his career as a seminary professor, so that his promotion found him ready for the new work that was assigned him.

The taking over of the Philippines from Spain by the United States after the Spanish-American War had involved the American authorities in a number of religious questions in the islands. The Spanish friars had converted the islanders some two to three centuries before, and as Chief Justice Taft declared after his visit to the Islands as Secretary of War under President Roosevelt had gradually lifted them up from barbarism. The Filipino insurrection however had brought embitterment against everything Spanish in the islands and the coming of the Americans made it utterly inadvisable to attempt to continue the régime of the Spanish bishops, in the Philippines. Within the first few years experience showed very clearly that if there was to be successful administration of the Church in the islands under the American protectorate the Spanish bishops would have to be replaced by Americans. Bishop Dougherty was the first American bishop to arrive in the archipelago and found himself compelled to take up the solution of the very important problems concerning Church matters which had become more and more involved and difficult of solution during the years since the transfer of the islands to the United States' authority.

By the direction of Pope Leo XIII Bishop Dougherty took with him to the Philippines five priests of the Philadelphia archdiocese who were to be professors at the diocesan seminary at Vigan in Nueva Segovia. This institution had been closed at the outbreak of the revolution against Spain but its immediate restoration was indispensable if native Filipinos were to be trained for the priesthood for service among their own people, which was the intention of the Roman authorities, as it has always been the policy of the Church. Almost needless to say these men faced very serious difficulties in the task thus presented to them at Vigan under the severe political conditions in the archipelago. Besides the climate was very trying for men from our latitude though of course the American priests had the example of the officers and men of our American troops who were submitted to similar conditions.

One of the five priests who went with Bishop Dougherty, Rev. Father Cook, died in Philadelphia a few years later a victim very probably to his apostolic zeal for the Church in the Philippines. The other four became bishops. Their names are worthy to be recalled because they represent the first great missionary effort beyond the boundaries of the United States of the secular priesthood of this country. They were the late Right Reverend James J. Carroll, promoted to the bishopric of Nueva Segovia where he succeeded Bishop Dougherty; Right Reverend John B. MacGinley, Bishop of Nueva Caceres in the Philippine Islands, afterwards transferred to Fresno, California; the third was Right Reverend James B. McCloskey, Bishop of Zamboanga in the Philippine Islands and afterwards the successor of Bishop Dougherty in the See of Jaro, Iloilo, P. I., and finally Right Reverend Daniel J. Gercke, Bishop of Tucson, Arizona.

As the American head of the diocese of Nueva Segovia, Bishop Dougherty found very much to do that had to be begun at once and continued energetically if his diocese was not to become rapidly more disorganized than he found it on his arrival. He rebuilt the façade of the cathedral which had been badly damaged by an earthquake and took up the problem of repairing and providing further buildings for the Catholic educational and charitable works of the diocese. The intellectual side of his duties as bishop were however much more important in his mind than the brick and mortar. He set about immediately restoring the diocesan seminary at Vigan; for a supply of native priests had to be secured without delay. The buildings of the seminary had been occupied by United States troops during the Filipino insurrection against the United States and almost inevitably under the circumstances had been greatly damaged. He set about making the repairs and reëstablishing the classes.

Bishop Dougherty realized the need of very definite missionary efforts among the Filipinos, especially now that they no longer had the advantage of the friars' labors in their regard and after the disturbances due to the Philippine insurrection and the Aglipayan schism. Accordingly he invited into the diocese the Belgian Missionaries of Scheut whose headquarters are near Brussels. Long ago Cæsar said after having been brought intimately in contact and fierce conflict with the people of Belgium, *fortissimi omnium sunt Belgae*—the bravest of them all are the Belgians. Such they have proved to be ever since and demonstrated the absolutely unchanging quality of the character of their people during the late War when the Belgians stood out so prominently before the world as the noblest hearted of all those on whom the burden of war was placed. Such they have been in the missionary fields all over the world and the trials and hardships of the Philippine missionary field were just what appealed to the indomitable spirit of courage in their work which is so characteristic of them.

As a fitting complement to the work of the Belgian missionaries an invitation was extended to the Fathers of the Divine Word whose mother house is at Steyl, Holland, and who have proved such worthy rivals of the Belgian missionaries all over the world. They are really Germans in origin but owing to the *Kulturkampf* this congregation of German priests was founded cross the German border in Holland and have proved the focus of attraction for a great many noble-hearted young German Catholics. Their work in the Philippines further exemplified their unselfish missionary zeal.

The success of both of these sets of missionaries amply justified Bishop Dougherty's invitation to them and his encouragement of their labors backed by their zealous efforts worked a veritable revolution in the feelings of the Filipinos with regard to the Church. Undoubtedly the work thus accomplished meant a very great deal for the renewal of devotion and adhesion to the old Church among the natives. If this missionary policy had not been initiated and followed up faithfully as it was a great many more of the natives would surely have been lost to the Church. As it was serious leaks were stopped.

After the Philadelphia priests were recalled home Bishop Dougherty invited the Jesuit fathers to take charge of the Vigan Seminary. It was particularly important that the younger Filipinos who felt the call to the priesthood should be thoroughly educated but also deeply grounded in their religion. It was extremely fortunate then that Bishop Dougherty was able to secure the Jesuits for this purpose. Before Bishop Dougherty came to the Philippines the Aglipayan schism had worked incalculable damage to religion. Whole sections of the diocese with native priests at the head of parishes joined the schism and had taken over Church properties. This caused intense confusion among the uneducated Filipinos and brought disturbance into the parish life of the natives in a great many places. A fervent priesthood had to be trained in order to take over the places that had been abandoned by schismatics and then arrangements had to be made to secure properties that would enable them to build up the Church once more in the districts where the schism had made itself felt most seriously.

There were many difficulties in the carrying out of this policy not the least of which were political because of the feelings that had been aroused among the natives and the effort of the local authorities to take advantage of the conditions in order to further foment religious troubles. On the plea that Church property belonged to the people, some of the municipalities throughout the Philippines had proceeded to usurp Church lands and Church buildings. This represented an opportunity for political corruption and for personal graft that was too good to be lost by local town officials.

In the confusion of the early efforts of the United States Government to bring about peace among the Filipinos the American authorities refused to correct these abuses, fearful of disturbing further native minds. Above all they refused to take any administrative action that would give back to the Catholic Church the properties of which they had formerly been the owners and compelled the ecclesiastical authorities to have recourse to legal processes to regain possession. This was slow and dilatory and the efforts of the Church to go on with its work among the people were hampered in many ways. All this required patience and tact and the bishop had to do the best that he could under the circumstances realizing that very probably it would be years before such legal processes could be brought to a definite and satisfactory conclusion.

As a matter of fact owing to the exigencies of politics in the United States the American government feared the political consequences of trying these cases until after many years. The intolerance with regard to Catholic questions which is so readily aroused in the United States, exemplified by the spread of the Ku Klux Klan even in our time, was twenty years ago even more sensitive to any possible hint of favor on the part of the United States government toward Catholics than it is at the present time. When the cases were tried in nearly every instance the Church won its cause, but by that time many of the Church buildings had been partly or wholly destroyed. The protracted and costly effort of thus securing once more the possession of Church holdings so absolutely necessary in order to carry on Church work effectively was an anxious and difficult task. To this the bishop was obliged to devote many years of his stay in the Philippines but any one who reads the story of the work that was thus successfully accomplished will appreciate better than could otherwise be possible the reasons why Church authorities should have felt that Bishop Dougherty deserved promotion. It was only a very proper recognition of his years of trying labor under missionary conditions that made the Roman authorities say to him after years, *Amice ascende superius,* "friend, go up higher."

After about five years in the diocese of Nueva Segovia, Bishop Dougherty was transferred to the Southern Islands and made Bishop of Jaro in the Province of Iloilo, P. I. While this was a more important diocese the work that he had to undertake was almost more difficult and involved great responsibilities and trials. In Jaro the Aglipayan schism had created veritable havoc and was the occasion of constant strife and never-ending abuses on the part of the schismatics. Bishop Dougherty succeeded in clearing up this very difficult situation very satisfactorily. He proved that he had the power and administrative ability that stamped him as the making of a great churchman and his work showed that he had a fount of energy for the service of the Church that was almost literally inexhaustible.

While bishop of Jaro, Bishop Dougherty com-

pleted the Jaro diocesan seminary. This was necessary in order to secure candidates for the ministry among the natives. The seminary had been
partially rebuilt by his predecessor, Bishop Rooker,
after it had been burned to the ground. Bishop
Dougherty felt however that the poor people must
be cared for and that besides the apostolic labors
of the missionaries there must be Christian charity
exercised for the benefit of the poor. In the town
of Iloilo, near Jaro, Bishop Dougherty built for the
purpose an up-to-date concrete hospital, one of the
largest in the East. Julian, whom the after-world
came to call the Apostate—had while emperor of
Rome—declared that the Christians' care for the
ailing poor gave them the strongest hold over the
populations among whom they lived. He even
added that until the old Olympic religion could
show similar proofs of beneficence for those in need,
it would be idle to attempt a restoration of the
old religion. Bishop Dougherty felt that hospital
work represented a bond between the Church authorities and the people stronger almost than any
other humanly speaking and therefore he was willing to make large sacrifices and devote some of his
best efforts to the creation and maintenance of this
magnificent hospital. It was placed in charge of
the Sisters of St. Paul of Chartres who conducted

it in thoroughly up-to-date fashion. At the town of Molo not far away from Jaro, Bishop Dougherty constructed a concrete orphanage so that the young Filipinos without parental care might be brought up as Christians and properly cared for. This orphanage was placed in charge of the Sisters of Charity.

Bishop Dougherty was very much interested here as he had been in Nueva Segovia in the education of young women so he invited to the diocese of Jaro the Sisters of the Assumption from France, who erected there and still conduct a high-class academy for young ladies.

Some idea of the extent to which Church properties had been destroyed during the Filipino insurrection against the United States may be gathered from the fact that the bishop's house in Jaro had been so utterly ruined as to be quite obliterated so that upon Archbishop Dougherty's arrival there not even the foundation could be traced. The restoration of this and of other Church properties was absolutely necessary not only for the dignity of the Church but also for the proper housing of Church activities. Shortly after his coming Bishop Dougherty secured for the diocese a bishop's residence in which the various functions of the diocese could be properly carried out. As in his former diocese of Nueva Segovia much of his time and attention had to be given to litigation over Church property. Advantage had been taken of every possible opportunity to expropriate Church property and use it for the benefit of the municipalities or for private purposes. Litigation was slow and protracted but had to be carried out in order to maintain the Church's right and establish precedents that would prevent further abuses.

These various restorations and foundations for the seminary, the hospital, the orphanage and the schools for young women required funds that in the disturbed state of the country after the revolution were very hard to secure in the Philippine Islands. During the years 1912, 1913 Bishop Dougherty spent a twelvemonth in the United States collecting from the good will of those who knew the excellent work that was being accomplished, the pecuniary resources that enabled him to continue the good work and its development and maintain the various institutions that had been established or refounded. He was extremely successful in this task and during the course of the next four years the diocese of Jaro came to be a model of its kind in the archipelago, one of those in which every provision was made for the proper provision of religious worship and charity and the maintenance of such good works as have always characterized Christianity.

It was not surprising then that after some twelve years in the Philippines, Bishop Dougherty was transferred to the flourishing diocese of Buffalo, New York. He came to the episcopacy of this important See after twenty-five years of significant preparation. A dozen of these years had been spent in the laborious task of professor at St. Charles Seminary, Overbrook, where his success had been the result of constant devotion to the work in hand. The next dozen years had been spent in the Philippines laboring at the difficult tasks of solving the serious problems connected with the change of government among a disaffected population where the bishop had to rebuild the church physically as well as spiritually in order to restore the influence which for centuries Catholicity had had upon the natives. Bishop Dougherty very soon made himself felt in the diocese of Buffalo. His chief material task there was to provide for the liquidation of the very large debt upon the new cathedral which had proved such a burden for his predecessor. His work in Buffalo was such as to indicate his administrative ability for a higher position, so after two years on May 1, 1918, he was made Archbishop of Philadelphia.

Back once more on his native heath in the archdiocese of Philadelphia the archbishop proceeded to
set the various works of his great archdiocese on a
firm footing and to reorganize the charities and
the educational institutions of Philadelphia so as
to make them as efficient as possible. Among the
works that he thus accomplished are the liquidation of the debt on St. Vincent's Orphanage, Lans-
downe, Pennsylvania, the conduction of financial
campaigns for the benefit of the Misericordia Hospital in which the Sisters of Mercy are doing such
good work in West Philadelphia and for the Houses
of the Good Shepherd of the Philadelphia diocese
which are accomplishing so much for the reformation of delinquents of various kinds among the
women. Then there came the establishment of St.
Mary's Institute for the Blind which was very much
needed, for Philadelphia had always been noted for
its special attention to all the problems relating to
the care of the blind. Other charitable foundations
followed. One of the most important was that of
the Italian Colombo Hospital in Philadelphia which
promises to be of so much service in taking care
of ailing poor among the Italians, for it is under
these circumstances particularly that their faith is
revived and an abiding sense of solidarity with
Catholicity produced. After that came the founda-

tion of the St. Francis Orphanage at Orwigsburg where the orphans of the diocese can be cared for out in the country, under the most healthful and pleasant conditions.

Education has however always been the special feature of Catholic work of the archdiocese of Philadelphia and Archbishop Dougherty proceeded to follow and expand the traditions that his great predecessors had established in this matter. For this purpose there came the erection of the faculty building and of a large annex of the West Philadelphia Catholic High School for Boys followed by the erection of the Northeast Catholic High School for Boys and of the West Philadelphia Catholic High School for Girls. In connection with these came the proper provision of early training for candidates for the priesthood through the erection of the preparatory seminary at Overbrook. All of these are either now in course of erection or are just finished. Besides under the patronage of Archbishop Dougherty there came the establishment of the Assumption Academy for Girls at Raven Hill and of the Grey Nuns' Academy at Melrose. In our day the education of young women is particularly important. Women are much more likely to be deeply influenced by their teachers than are our young men for it has been said by one of our great secular university presidents—that one of the happiest traits of young men is their power to shed unfortunate influences in education very much in the same way that a duck sheds water. The provision of thoroughly conservative education for young women is particularly important—as is well illustrated by some of the radicalism that has found its way into colleges for young women in this country.

A typical instance of Cardinal Dougherty's interest in Catholic higher education for young women is afforded by the foundation of the academy of Miraflores in Peru. The Peruvian archbishop realizing the need for Catholic higher education for women and the advisability of having Catholic teachers of English, turned to his colleague of Philadelphia whose experience in the Philippines had made him so sympathetic toward the problems of Spanish bishops, and asked for help in the matter. Cardinal Dougherty turned to the Congregation of the Sisters of the Immaculate Heart of Mary who have done so much for education in the archdiocese of Philadelphia, and asked that they should send a community to Peru. A group of sisters volunteered for the purpose and their work has been eminently successful. In the course of three years they have gathered round them some two hundred students for whom a new building has been completed on Avenida Leguia that is said to be ideal for the purpose. The President of Peru and the Minister of Education were present at the dedication of the building and the medal struck for the commemoration of the event has the names of the President and the Reverend Mother Superior as memorials of the international occasion.

While thus devoting himself to the charitable and educational needs of his great archdiocese, the Archbishop of Philadelphia appreciated very thoroughly the necessity for providing for the direct spiritual necessities of his people. It was particularly important to make it not only possible but easy for all the members of the Church to perform their spiritual duties without difficulty. The archbishop has brought about for this purpose the establishment of some sixty-four new parishes in his diocese so that there are very few places where the members of the Church cannot attend Mass and receive the Sacraments without any special inconvenience or any great effort being required.

After a record like this of Church work it is not surprising that some three years after his appointment as Archbishop of Philadelphia, in the early spring of 1921, Archbishop Dougherty was raised to the cardinalate by Pope Benedict XV.

One of the most significant phases of special interest in Cardinal Dougherty's life and one that deserves to be mentioned because it serves to illuminate the culmination of his career as a churchman very strikingly is his devotion to her whom Catholics love to call "The Little Flower." This is the loving name given to the recently canonized (April, 1925) Saint Thérèse Martin of Lisieux in France. She was only twenty-four when she died and had spent more than one-third of that brief life behind the grille of a Carmelite convent. In spite of this fact which would seem to make it impossible that within twenty-five years after her death she should be known all over the world, her name is more often mentioned everywhere throughout Catholicity than that of any other woman of modern times. It is probably true to say that during the year since her canonization as a saint more statues of her have been set up than of any other woman except the Mother of the Lord. The reason for all this reverence and admiration is not easy to find if one looks at the worldly side of it. Little Thérèse, as she loved to call herself, did no great things from a worldly standpoint. Her life was mystically hidden with Christ but was so strikingly beautiful that it has caught the attention of all the world who have come to know anything about her.

Her wonderfully simple life and single-hearted devotion to prayer for the benefit of others made her long before her cult was so widely propagated— as it is at the present time a favorite subject of devotion on the part of the Cardinal of Philadelphia. As a result of that he has become one of the most distinguished promoters of her cult. She represents above all the type of saintship represented by those who are ready to give up everything that might come to them, even their heavenly reward if only thus they would secure the salvation of others. It is said that St. Ignatius Loyola once said that if it were the Will of God and would redound to His glory he would be willing to be damned. What the Little Flower said went not quite so far as that though at the moment of her death she declared, "I feel that my mission is about to commence. My mission is to make God loved as I love Him, to point out to souls my little way. I wish to pass my Heaven in doing good on earth. No, I shall never be able to take any rest until the very end of the world; but when the angels shall have said, 'Time is no more'—then I shall take my rest, for the number of the elect will be then completed."

The very fact that the distinguished cardinal of a great archdiocese the course of whose life in many and various positions had demonstrated his capacity as a scholar, his ability as an administrator, his missionary zeal, under the most difficult circumstances, his attention to detail in those practical affairs of existence, should be thus devoted to the Little Flower of Lisieux is indeed interesting as a revelation of the interior spirit of the man.   As a professor of theology in one of the best known of our seminaries, as a bishop in the Philippines under the most trying circumstances, as an American prelate ruling an important populous diocese, and finally as the archbishop of one of the greatest Catholic Sees in the world and as a cardinal of the universal Church, he has exhibited the most practical qualities, but in this devotion to the Little Flower there is a glimpse of the mystical side of the man and of his spiritual ardor.   The fact that the Little Flower has been canonized when scarcely more than half the number of years have passed since her death that are under ordinary circumstances required by Canon Law is the proof that Cardinal Dougherty's sentiment in the matter is manifestly in harmony with the spirit of the Church.

He had made his diocese a fountainhead of devotion to this little woman, scarcely more than a girl, whom the Church has just raised to the altars because of the profound simplicity and self-abnegation of her character. The sympathy that has created devotion to her in a few years all over the world shows how profoundly Catholic is the reverence for her which Cardinal Dougherty was one of the first high-placed ecclesiastics to take up and encourage. The life of the youthful Carmelite seems scarcely significant enough from a worldly standpoint to deserve such attention as is thus given to it, but the real significance of the life of man is from within and not without. Thomas à Kempis treats of the interior life almost exclusively in his *Following of Christ* which consists after all only of a set of conferences given to the novices of his order and yet his little book has been the most published volume except the Bible all over the world for these 450 years since his death. Our oldest university, Harvard, was willing to spend a large sum of money in order to secure a series of books about à Kempis though that little man lived some seventy-three years in the monastery of St. Agnes scarcely ever leaving the grounds of the monastery and yet seeing the meaning of life so clearly that 450 years later his little book is still one of the most precious that humanity has.

The little Thérèse of Lisieux like her sister Carmelite of over three hundred years before, the great St. Teresa of Spain, has demonstrated how much the contemplative life can mean in producing a deep and lasting effect on the world in which it lives. It has often been said that St. Teresa of Spain from behind her convent grille kept back the tide of the Reformation in Spain. That enabled Spain to accomplish wonderful work just at the time when most of the nations of Europe were so sadly disturbed by the religious feuds almost universally occurring that their power of achievement was at its lowest ebb. Spain's golden century of literature, art, architecture and the arts and crafts came just after the Reformation and the Spanish Carmelite St. Teresa was a marvelous factor for its success and its supreme prestige. It has been suggested that in our time when the material world is encroaching so sadly on the spiritual and making life all too sordid, that the example and the influence of the Little Flower, St. Thérèse of our day, may serve to turn back the tide of irreligion or at least greatly help in this direction and thus provide an opportunity for another great period of spiritual, artistic and æsthetic achievement. If this should happen Cardinal Dougherty's early interest in the Little Flower will have meant much for the new order of things.

Philadelphia is one of the greatest Catholic archdioceses in the world. It is among the very first

in the number of its Catholic inhabitants but above
all in the fine organization of the Church within its
bounds. It has a magnificent group of Catholic
charitable institutions of all kinds; orphan asylums,
hospitals, corrective institutions and the like, and
supremely well organized schools and high schools
as well as colleges and seminaries. It is very probable that in practical Catholicity as measured by
attendance at the Church and Sacraments in proportion to the whole number of Catholics, Philadelphia stands out as one of the excelling archdioceses
of the Catholic Church. For long it was the largest city in the country at the beginning of the history of the United States but it has continued to
grow constantly and persistently and its conservatism has done much to foster the Church and its
growth. It is true that here the Know-Nothing
riots were at their worst and churches and convents
burned, but after that spasm of intolerance Philadelphia has continued to be a very favorable setting for the continuous growth of the Church. It
was to this promising diocese that Bishop Dougherty after his missionary experience in the Philippines and the further development of character and
demonstration of ability that came with the important See of Buffalo was sent by his ecclesiastical
superiors in Rome because they felt that here was

a man who had accomplished difficult tasks and high purposes and who could surely be trusted to bear heavier burdens and achieve even more difficult work.

After his elevation to the archiepiscopacy it was only a question of time and opportunity to show his adequacy to the new tasks that had been placed on him before the conferment of the cardinal's hat placed him in the highest rank of Catholic ecclesiastics of the world, next to the Pope. There is no doubt at all that under his archiepiscopacy Philadelphia will continue to grow more Catholic not only in numbers but in spirit. The magnificent organization of education and of charity makes the Church stand out as one of the most important of factors for the making of better citizens. They are sadly needed at the present time when crime is so much more common in our country than it is in any other civilized country in the world, and there seems no doubt that it will not be long before there will come general recognition on the part of all the citizens of the country of the work that the Catholic Church is doing in this regard and Philadelphia is one of the leaders.

GEORGE, CARDINAL MUNDELEIN

Sixth American Cardinal

Cardinal George William Mundelein was born July 2, 1872, on the lower East Side of New York City not far away from where his colleague in the American cardinalate, Cardinal Hayes, was born only a few years before, and where Governor Smith of New York State was born the following year. A circle with a diameter of less than half a mile would include the birth places of all three of these men who have impressed themselves so deeply on their generation and reached distinction in their chosen careers. He was the son of Francis and Mary (Goetz) Mundelein who were of German descent but they and their parents had resided in America for many years and were profoundly American in feeling. The best possible evidence for this is to be found in the fact that his grandfather was one of the first to enlist when Lincoln's call for troops to defend the Union came in the very early days of the Civil War, and he was the first man killed in the Union ranks at the Battle of Fort Sumter.

The death of his grandfather leaving a large family of children with no income to provide for them made life rather trying for the Mundeleins in that and the next generation so that the family circumstances were rather straitened in the early years of the cardinal's boyhood. As a result he had the advantage of that training which Thucydides insisted was the best possible for growing youth—having to go through hard things when one is young —which the great Greek historian declared lifts a man above the great mass of mankind if he has anything in him really worth while.

The boy who was later to be the Cardinal Archbishop of Chicago learned from personal experience all the trials of narrow circumstances. There probably never was a time in his early life, once he grew out of actual infancy, when George Mundelein did not have certain work to do around the home that it was necessary for him to do. Straitened though life was for them by their rather difficult conditions of life, his folks were resolved to give him just as good an education as they could and no sacrifice was too much for them to make for that purpose. At the age of six he was sent not to the public free school but to St. Nicholas parish school not far from his home in New York, where at that time his parents would be expected to make a definite con-

CARDINAL MUNDELEIN

tribution to the expenses of his education. He succeeded very well at the school and attracted the attention of his teachers—the good Sisters of St. Dominic, who encouraged him to go on and secure an education for he had the ability that would make sacrifices for that purpose worth while. There is still a good Sister at the old St. Nicholas parochial school who remembers him very well as a boy there and tells how faithful he was at his studies and how excellent he was in his conduct.

He needed very little encouragement, however, to take advantage to the best possible extent of whatever opportunities for education might be provided for him, for from his earliest years he was ambitious to acquire knowledge. On the other hand his folks were ever ready to continue to do anything and everything that might be necessary in order that he should have the chance to develop his mind. As a consequence of this, after graduating from the parochial school he was sent to old De La Salle Institute on Second Street in New York City where the Brothers of the Christian Schools founded in Paris by John Baptist de la Salle some 250 years ago were engaged in affording so many of the sons of the lower East Side families their introduction to higher education. The centuries of tradition behind them in education were very precious for the work of bringing out all that was in the boys. Many after personal experience in their schools were quite ready to declare in later life that they felt that there are no teachers like these Christian Brothers for real development of mind and the awakening of intellectual interests. They succeeded admirably in arousing their scholars' own ambition to learn and they were willing to sacrifice any time and attention that will help on that purpose. Often their own free days and hours are given over by the good Brothers to their pupils and they become their personal friends in such ways as prove wonderful incentives to study and the acquisition of knowledge. Many a young man of that time in New York owed his best possible preparation for life to the solid study following a very definite curriculum, every item of which was required, without any elective features, under the methods of the Brothers of the Christian Schools.

Just as the future cardinal was beginning his high-school work in old De La Salle Institute, owing to the military strain in the family and the fact that his grandfather had been killed in the service of the United States, he was urged by a number of his friends to enter West Point where a cadetship was open to him. But already he had felt the call to the priesthood and so he prepared to enter the service of the Church confident that in this way he would be fulfilling his patriotic as well as religious duties.

The memory of himself that George Mundelein left behind at De La Salle Institute as we gather it from some of those who knew him in the distant school days, was that of a very quiet, studious youth, most unobtrusive in his ways, faithful in every duty, never getting into trouble, and making himself liked by everyone by his simplicity and kindness. Many of the boys lingered after school for a time for games among themselves and sometimes for talks with the teachers, but young Mundelein almost never did, because he had too many things at home to occupy him and many chores to be done, so as to do his share in family life, since they were doing so much for him.

At De La Salle he first came in contact with the future Archbishop of New York, Patrick J. Hayes, who was later to receive on the same day with him, at the hands of the Pope, the cardinalitial dignity. After he had completed his high-school work he entered Manhattan College where Cardinal Hayes also received his college education under the tutelage of the Christian Brothers. Here they came to know each other very well and when their fellow students of that time marched in the procession that greeted them as they sailed for Rome to be made cardinals they reminded them of that earlier day when they had just been plain George and Pat to each other and to so many others.

After fruitful years at Manhattan College where he received his degree of A.B. at twenty the future Cardinal of Chicago went out to pursue his philosophical studies at St. Vincent's College, Beatty, Pa. Here the Benedictines some fifty years before had laid the foundations of a great abbey connected with which was a college and theological seminary. The monastic seclusion of St. Vincent's situated as it was far from bustling city life and in surroundings resembling those which had characterized the first foundations of the Benedictines, when their great founder began that withdrawal from "the madding crowd" which meant so much for the cultivation of letters in an unfavorable time, made it a place where true education in the sense of the chance to think out thoughts as they come, might be secured. St. Benedict, almost unconsciously to himself, had thus laid the foundation of the Monks of the West. St. Vincent's modern counterpart of Monte Cassino proved to be a home of culture and the intellectual life in that more distant west beyond the ocean undreamt of in St. Benedict's day. The impress of those Benedictine years is probably still noticeable in the disci-

pline of Cardinal Mundelein's life and the serious-
ness of his outlook on great intellectual problems.

At the age of twenty the young neophyte preparing for the priesthood, after the preliminary courses
in life as it is lived on the lower East Side of New
York and under the fine traditions of the Christian
Brothers and the Benedictines, set out for Rome
where for three years more he pursued his course
at the College of Propaganda.

On June 8, 1895, George Mundelein was ordained
to the priesthood not by one of the distinguished
Roman cardinals as is usually the case with those
who study in Rome and are ordained there, but by
his own Bishop McDonnell, not in one of the great
basilicas but in the chapel of the Sisters of the Holy
Cross. He celebrated his first mass the following
day in the crypt of St. Peter's. The intimate relations between his bishop and himself which had begun with his adoption as a seminarian and his transfer to Rome for his major studies in theology and
which culminated in his ordination, were continued
after his return to the United States by his appointment as assistant secretary to the bishop. For a few
months as a young priest he had pastoral charge of
the Lithuanian Church in the Eastern District of
Brooklyn, although he remained attached to the
household of the bishop. The only parochial duties

that Cardinal Mundelein ever performed were those which came to him as rector of the cathedral chapel, Queen of All Saints, Brooklyn, in connection with his position in the bishop's household. It was to his initiative however that was due the building of this chapel as it is called, though it is really a large church. He also built the parish school in connection with the cathedral parish and these two buildings have been proclaimed striking examples of how beautiful Gothic architecture can be applied to modern ecclesiastical structures. Later he built the Church of Our Lady of the Isle at Long Beach, another beautiful building.

After a brief two years, in December, 1897, he was appointed chancellor of the diocese of Brooklyn an office which he held for some twelve years until he was made the auxiliary bishop of the Brooklyn diocese. Cardinal Mundelein's work was worthy of this recognition and five years after he became chancellor further recognition came in his appointment as a Censor of the Liturgical Academy, November, 1903. Three years later (1906) he was made a domestic prelate to the Pope with the title of Monsignor, one of the youngest on whom the honor has been conferred, in recent years at least. The following year for a brilliant defense of Pope Pius X's condemnation of modernism he was made a member of the Ancient Academy of Arcadia, one of the learned academies of Rome. This honor had never come to America before.

Manifestly Rome was keeping its eye on the young chancellor of the Brooklyn diocese for the very next year while representing the diocese of Brooklyn at the Pope's jubilee he was granted the degree of Doctor of Sacred Theology by the Congregation of the Propaganda. As a student of the Urban College of the Propaganda, he was looked upon as one of her sons whose careers would always have the watchful eye of alma mater on them.

In 1909 he was selected as Auxiliary Bishop of Brooklyn and on September 21st of that year he was consecrated as titular bishop of Laryma, one of the episcopal sees of ancient Christianity which had lost its episcopal dignity because of the decrease in population. Earlier the same year the bishops of the province had selected him as their candidate for the vacant bishopric of Louisville, Kentucky. A destiny in the hierarchy of the United States was evidently preparing for him. As Auxiliary Bishop of Brooklyn he was appointed director of the Cathedral College of the Immaculate Conception of the diocese. This was the preparatory or "little seminary" as it is called in which boys who aspire to the priesthood are given the special secular education in connection with religious studies and exercises that will fit them for their further curriculum in philosophy and theology in the theological seminary and prepare them for the fulfillment of the duties required of them in their vocation as priests. Undoubtedly it was his successful organization of this college and his wise regulation of it as its first rector which led to the recognition of his administrative ability and suggested his suitability for the vacant position of Archbishop of Chicago. This demanded a man of tried prudence and capacity for organization and such Bishop Mundelein had proved himself to be. He was the youngest archbishop in the country though Chicago was the second largest and most populous archdiocese. He had begun his advancement in the hierarchy by being the youngest of domestic prelates to the Pope so that unprecedented distinctions for his years were no longer a surprise.

Those in Chicago who were acquainted with the newly appointed archbishop at once proclaimed their confidence that his appointment would mean very much for the development and reorganization of the great archdiocese of the Middle West. Rev. John M. Bowen who had been a classmate in Rome of the newly appointed archbishop when questioned by a reporter of one of the Chicago papers said, "I remember Bishop Mundelein as an extremely scholarly young man. Even in those days he was known as one of the most popular students among us. He knew every one. As a young man he was active —unusually so, a characteristic which I understand still marks him. Above all his other attributes the one characteristic which stands out most clearly in my memory is his passion for study and his remarkable knowledge along lines ecclesiastical."

Right Reverend Monsignor Francis C. Kelley, the director of the Catholic Church Extension Society of the United States, whose headquarters are in Chicago and whose own executive ability had made that society a wonderful force for the spread of Catholicity in the United States, declared "He is going to win his way into our hearts—I can say that with perfect confidence. I know him and he has that faculty—he gives his whole heart and soul to his work."

The welcome accorded him as archbishop by both the clergy and the laity of Chicago was such as to provide ample assurance of the loyalty and fidelity of his flock. It became perfectly clear that a new era for the development of the great archdiocese whose diocesan city was the metropolis of the Middle West, was about to open. As Father Bowen had said of him as a student, it was not long before people began to like him very much and his activity proved an incentive to others that very soon made the diocese bustling with church interests of all kinds. His popularity grew from the very beginning and it was not long before he came to be looked up to as a father and a friend by all those who were brought in any way intimately in touch with him.

His promotion to the See of Chicago came in December, 1915, so that now he has been more than a decade of years at the head of that great archdiocese. The record of his achievement in this position of responsibility and hard work necessitating the fulfillment of so many administrative details and the solution of so many important problems, makes it very clear that the ecclesiastical authorities made no mistake in choosing him for this exalted dignity with all the burdens that it involves. Already though still a comparatively young man he has accomplished so much that there is no doubt left in the minds of any who know him that if spared he will leave in the course of time a wonderfully organized archdiocese in which every feature of Catholic life will be developed to the point where it can most deeply influence for good all the people, Catholic and Protestant, within the limits of the archdiocese. His sterling qualities of mind and heart and soul have stilled certain dissentient diocesan elements present in former times and have brought a union and harmony of effort among the clergy that is producing strikingly good effects upon the people.

At the time of his translation from Brooklyn to Chicago, he was hailed as the youngest archbishop in America and probably in the world. His years, however, proved only an excuse for the exertion of more energy in the affairs of the great archdiocese of Chicago and not at all for hesitancy of action. His activities proved so far from anything like imprudent that it was not long before the youthful archbishop had attracted the attention of prominent citizens of Chicago and had secured their entire confidence. As a result he has taken a place in the religious, economic, patriotic, educational and civic life of Chicago that has redounded to the glory of the Church and given her the place that she deserves in the city's existence since so many of the citizens of Chicago belong to the Church's fold. After all, in Chicago Archbishop Mundelein is the spiritual head of nearly 1,500,000 people comprising some thirty nationalities. He is the principal instrument through which they find a voice in the social life of the great metropolis of the West. No wonder then that as a worthy leader, prominent men in every line

of thought have learned to look to his pronouncements and have sought to find out his opinion on all
matters of importance even those which are quite
outside the ordinary domain of his interest as a
churchman.

It was thought in Chicago that very probably one
of the first tasks which their young energetic archbishop would assume would be that of building a
great new cathedral worthy of the metropolis of
the West. This was one of the earliest suggestions
that came to him and for a time it was entertained
as representing very probably the first great step in
the new policy of the archdiocesan administration.
It gave way in the archbishop's mind before long to
his desire to relieve just as far as possible the sufferings and disadvantages of poverty among his people. His own broad experience of life made him
realize very poignantly how much of need there was
for thorough-going organization for improving the
condition of the poor and helping them to help themselves, as well as preventnig the immediate sufferings due to the want of absolute necessities of life.

As the archbishop himself said, "I would rather
uplift the poor and despairing to a better and happier life than rear the greatest cathedral in the
world." He called together a group of the wealth-
iest and most influential Catholics of the archdiocese

not for the purpose of organizing for the building of a cathedral but for the foundation of the Associated Catholic Charities of the archdiocese of Chicago. This organization collects and distributes annually nearly a million of dollars in charity and it has done much to solve the most urgent problems of poverty in the archdiocese.

Certain features of the organization of charity show how thoughtfully the program has been developed. The Misericordia Maternity Hospital for charity cases erected at a cost of nearly $200,000 and maintained by funds granted annually from the Associated Catholic Charities is capable of caring for one hundred mothers and their babies. One of the phases of maternity hospital work in the modern time that sometimes is disturbing is the fact that the life of the child is not always held of just as high value as that of the mother. During our generation a great many lives of infants have been deliberately sacrificed because the sacrifice saved some pain and discomfort to the mothers, or because it was thought to lessen the risk of life to which mothers might be subjected. It is easy to understand then, why, when this maternity hospital was erected His Grace gave as the reason for it "for the saving of the souls of the babies." Special precautions are taken to secure in every possible instance the baptism of the child and to maintain its right to life as quite equal to that of its mother.

Another outcome of this same fatherly solicitude for those who need the help of others because of the conditions in which they find themselves placed was the reorganization of the system of employment of the young women detained at the House of Good Shepherd. This is an institution under the direction of the Sisters of the Good Shepherd founded some two hundred years ago in France for the care of wayward girls. Archbishop Mundelein brought about the organization of a system of employment of the "children," as they are called by the Sisters, with pay and in connection with a savings fund. As a result of this the girls when discharged from detention are sure to have sufficient funds to maintain themselves if it should be necessary for them to be idle for a time before finding occupation at the particular kind of employment in which they became proficient during their stay at the home. This plan has worked very wonderfully and has made the girls independent of circumstances to a degree that has enabled hundreds of them to continue to lead good lives without hardship, even though they meet with serious disappointments in the matter of finding appropriate employment.

Archbishop Mundelein was particularly anxious

that the orphans of his great archdiocese should be properly cared for. His solicitude in this matter led to the development and extension of the facilities of the St. Mary's Training and Industrial Schools at Desplaines, Illinois. Here orphan boys and girls are taught self-supporting trades. They are trained for their work at these and in connection with a wage and saving system are taught thrift and at the same time made capable of taking care of themselves when they are ready to go out into the world. With this work plans have been developed for the erection of a large orphan home near Lockport, Illinois, to cost in the neighborhood of one million dollars. This will accommodate the orphans of Will and Grundy Counties and special provision will be made for the training of young folks whose interests will mainly be those of the country and the farming districts in the hope that this may prove a factor in preventing the ever continued migration from country to city which is crowding the city and making life artificial and superficial. This is all the more important because the number of the producers of the necessaries of life is constantly on the decrease with the prospect of serious results in the one-sided development of life that seems almost inevitable, unless definite efforts are made to train the young for an agricultural career.

After the organization of the charities of his archdiocese his next care was for education. The education of the clergy was the most important foundation stone for that purpose. One of the earliest works Archbishop Mundelein set himself to was the organization of the "little seminary" or preparatory school for the ecclesiastical seminary in Chicago. His experience as the first rector and organizer of the Cathedral College of the Immaculate Conception in Brooklyn had given him valuable training in this matter, and so it is not surprising that Quigley Preparatory Seminary, so called in honor of his distinguished predecessor who planned for it, was an immediate success. Its success has been emphasized with the years. At the present time there are some eight hundred students in attendance at it.

While so many of the religious sects in this country are complaining of the difficulty that they have in securing candidates for the ministry, the Catholic Church finds no such difficulty but secures without trouble almost larger numbers of aspirants for the priesthood than are needed. This has proved particularly true in Chicago under Cardinal Mundelein's fostering care though there had been some dearth of candidates before and Chicago had secured her priests from many parts of the world as well as from among her own people. The training afforded these young men at the preparatory seminary is well calculated to develop their vocation as ministers of the Gospel and their fidelity and loyalty as priests of the archdiocese of Chicago, as well as make them ready for their sacerdotal life work in such a way as will render them most valuable in the service of the Church for the benefit of their country.

After the "little seminary" was thus well organized the archbishop planned at once the foundation of a major seminary where the candidates to the priesthood for the Chicago archdiocese could be properly taught and trained for their life work. He recognized the advantage of life in the country both because of the health and the lack of distraction from studies that it insured. Accordingly the seminary was located on a large tract of land in the little town of Area some thirty miles north of Chicago. The district in which the seminary is located has since been called Mundelein in his honor. The seminary itself is called St. Mary's of the Lake because it is situated at the head of a lake which is entirely included in the seminary property. This has afforded a fine opportunity for landscape gardening and for pleasant shaded walks on rising ground that surrounds the lake. These cross bridges over arms of the lake at several points. All this adds very much to the beauty of the grounds and makes the seminary property one of the most charming of its kind anywhere in the world. As a result of the attention devoted to it, it has become an extremely suitable place for young men during their impressionable years to spend time that can scarcely help but refine their taste and give them a proper sense of artistic settings for Church property.

The architecture of this seminary has widely attracted the attention of Catholics in the United States who are interested in the Church's relationship to the nation. By Archbishop Mundelein's suggestion the lines of the chapel which occupies a central position among the seminary buildings were planned to follow the Colonial style of Church architecture which had been developed here in America in the Colonial days. As a boy he had passed some summers near Lyme in Connecticut and had been deeply impressed by the old-fashioned meeting-house of that little town. He instructed the architect to pattern after this and sent him to study it in its original location. This is what has been reproduced very beautifully as the central unit of the seminary buildings. The symbolism of this style is meant to emphasize the intimate relation between Catholicism and Americanism. It has been suggested that this is putting a holy water font in a

Protestant meeting-house and that they are incompatible, but the effect produced has been very striking and grows on one the more that is seen of it. The seminary buildings are planned to accord with this and they constitute a very impressive group of structures.

Almost inevitably the adoption of this style has attracted a great deal of attention and has proved a subject of ardent discussion. Many do not hesitate to say that the putting aside of older styles of ecclesiastical architecture in favor of this very modern mode of structural expression is of dubious value. They insist that the Colonial mode of construction does not lend itself to such expression of serious religious ideas as is worthy of so important an edifice. On the other hand there are many who feel that the symbolism of the union between Americanism and Catholicism so well emphasized by dedicating what seems externally a Protestant chapel to the service of Catholic worship is well worth the effort that has been expended on it. After all the Church has always adopted and adapted whatever was found good in the countries and among the peoples to whom she came. She has not always imposed her way of looking at things, but has constantly dedicated national ideas to Church service. In this sense the chapel at Mundelein expresses the intimate thought of our time and the feelings and sentiments of the builders in the same way that the old architecture expressed the thoughts and aspirations of the ages of faith. The severer lines of the Colonial architecture emphasize above all the austerity of justice which represents the core of Anglo-Saxon contribution to modern civilization and justice is one of the greatest of the attributes of God.

The buildings out at St. Mary's of the Lake represent the last word in construction so far as ventilation, sanitation and convenience are concerned. They are thoroughly fireproof and are so arranged that noise is not transmitted and the best possible surroundings for study are created. The grouping of the buildings alongside of the chapel on the higher ground above the end of the lake is extremely effective and they are surrounded by grounds that are marvelously beautiful. Some fifty thousand plants are put out each spring and in their growth they produce a wonderful effect. The landscape architect chosen with as much care as the construction architect has been given full opportunity to bring out all the natural beauty of the scene and he has succeeded very wonderfully. The walks and roads and paths are all so placed as to add to the beauty rather than detract from it and are carried out so as to represent certain boundary lines for various portions of the ground rather than utilitarian necessities that had to be inserted into the landscape. The landing at the edge of the lake has been treated so finely as to add greatly to the charm of the scene and the whole result is indeed a thing of beauty that cannot help but be a joy forever.*

Archbishop Mundelein was intent, however, not alone on education for the priesthood but also on Catholic religious training for all ages of the young people of his diocese who were to spend their lives doing the practical work of the world. Parochial school education was taken up by Archbishop Mundelein and carried forward with characteristic thoroughness and prevision. Some idea of the work

---

*The Cardinal has very wisely chosen to make the scene of the great procession of the Blessed Sacrament for the Eucharistic Congress the grounds of St. Mary's of the Lake. Here there are four miles of walks around the lake crossing bridges over arms of the lake at various points that will make a wonderful setting for the Eucharistic procession. It will be possible to see every portion of the procession from any part of it. Very probably never has so suitable a location been found for so huge a religious procession as this will prove to be. As an immense crowd, probably approaching a million of people if not more, will find their way to Chicago for the Eucharistic Congress, the beautiful grounds will make a rare sight for them and will add greatly to the impressiveness of the scene. It is probable that those who visit the seminary grounds at that time will never forget them. The background of lake and trees and sky and the striking group of seminary buildings always in view will make the scene one of the most beautiful ever witnessed. The Eucharistic Congress has never probably had a more striking background.

that was accomplished will be obtained from the fact that in the 239 city parishes of Chicago itself according to the latest directory 220 have parochial schools. Only a very definite understanding that opportunities for Catholic education must be provided in every parish could have brought about a result of this kind. His care, however, was not only for the provision of the schools themselves but also for affording such education in them as would leave as far as possible nothing to be desired. The quality of the education was his special solicitude. As a consequence he insisted on the closer grading of the parochial schools and the direction by the diocesan board of every detail of education with the standardization of courses of study and of textbooks. He emphasized above all that special attention must be given to necessary subjects and that the basis of all teaching be English and that thoroughly American love of country be the watchword in the training of young Catholic citizens.

This system has been further perfected by the creation of a board of school visitors and of supervisors composed of priests especially educated and trained for the work. Since the Church is assuming the responsibility for the elementary education of the children of Catholics, it must organize so as to provide the best possible education for the children. They must be in a position to secure all that they would be able to obtain in public schools so far as real education is concerned and then besides they must have the benefit of religious training.

This was only the beginning, however, and after the grammar-school reorganization, indeed simultaneously with it, came the reorganization of the Catholic high schools of the city. As the result of Archbishop Mundelein's urgent insistence on the development of this phase of the Catholic school system, there has come into existence a series of district high schools for Catholics worthy of the Church and of the religious education that she is fostering. Every step in the systematization of these high schools has been made only after consultation with recognized authorities in pedagogy and the according of their fullest approval of the plans. Indeed the special characteristic of this development has been the care exercised to be sure that nothing should be attempted that had not been well weighed and considered by those of expert authority in education.

A number of these schools are already in operation. Immaculata High School on the North Side, Mercy High School on the South Side, the Josephinum High School in northwest Chicago, Alverno High School on the Northwest Side, the Mallin-

krodt in Wilmette and the Catholic High School in
Waukegan are examples. Those more recently built
like Mercy and Alverno High Schools are million-
dollar plants capable of accommodating very con-
veniently a thousand pupils each. They have both
been opened in the last few years and are filled to
capacity. They furnish the best assurance that further development of this high-school system will
prove a boon to the Catholic population of Chicago.
The plan is to cover the entire city with these district Catholic high schools for girls. When the system is completed there will be twelve of them in all.
High schools for boys are planned to correspond
with these to be erected according to the needs
within the next few years. There has been a great
increase in the number of young people seeking
higher education beyond the elementary studies in
Chicago and the cardinal has encouraged this in
every way and his heart is more deeply wrapped up
in the provision of education for all, education of
the heart as well as of the head, than almost anything else.

The cardinal's plans include, moreover, not only
the reorganization of grammar and high-school
education but also of collegiate and university education. All of the Catholic colleges and universities
have been coördinated in such a way as to secure the

highest efficiency. The central unit of the great Catholic University of Chicago is the seminary at Mundelein, Ill. The seminary faculty is already organized with diocesan priests occupying the administrative positions and the Jesuits as professors. More than 250 students are pursuing courses in philosophy and theology, and though one of the youngest of the seminaries in the country it has already come to be looked upon as one of the best organized. Only those who are studying for the exercise of the ministry of the priesthood in Chicago are admitted to the seminary and this gives a solidarity and a unity of heart to all that promises well for their future coöperation in the work of the Church in Chicago. The lack of a diocesan seminary has been rather seriously felt in the past; because of the effect that might be expected from it the prospect is bright indeed for the training of clergymen who will work well together.

Archbishop Mundelein was very much interested not only in higher education for young men but also for young women. Not long after his arrival in Chicago he invited the Dominican Sisters who had for a long generation been so successful in the higher education of women at Sinsinawa in Wisconsin to open a college in the neighborhood of Chicago. They had already proceeded to college work at the old site which was, however, not suited for modern developments in higher education. A large tract of land was procured at River Forest west of Chicago and plans were formed for the expenditure of over a million of dollars for the erection of suitable buildings. Ralph Adams Cram, the distinguished Boston architect, was chosen as the architect of the new structures and the result is a marvelously beautiful group of buildings bearing about them all the old monastic traditions and yet thoroughly up to date in their provision of the most modern facilities. Cloisters are charmingly medieval, but close alongside them is a very modern swimming pool and the same interesting contrast of what is beautiful in the olden times mingled with what is thoroughly convenient in the present day is to be noted everywhere throughout the buildings. Rosary College, as it is called, now has some three hundred students in attendance and its affiliation with the Catholic University of Chicago under the ægis of the archbishop, gives it the prospect of magnificent success in the near future.

At the same time there came a corresponding development among the Sisters of Mercy, the religious congregation that had for so many years been one of the great founts of good work in both education and charity for the archdiocese of Chi-

cago.   Down at Forty-seventh and Cottage Grove
Avenue St. Francis Xavier's College was founded
and developed by them and afforded an excellent
opportunity for young women to secure a college
education without having to leave their homes if
they lived in Chicago. At the same time it provided
excellent facilities for the sisters themselves to enable their younger sisters to secure the higher education under religious auspices. Under such circumstances religious vocations are fostered and young
women come eagerly to take up the life-work of devoting themselves to Christian education and charity. The work of the Sisters of Mercy in this regard has made them very well known by all who
are interested in the elevation of human minds and
hearts and souls to what is best in them. At the
Mercy Hospital in Chicago, Dr. John B. Murphy
for many years did some of the best work in surgery
that, according to his American and English colleagues, was done anywhere in the world for this
last three hundred years. There can be no doubt
then of the ability of the Sisters of Mercy to organize modern institutions up to the needs of the hour
and this Cardinal Mundelein recognizes and has
encouraged in every way.

On March 2, 1925, cablegrams were sent from
Rome to the Archbishops of Chicago and New

York, summoning them to Rome, there to be clothed
with the dignity of cardinals. Archbishop Mundelein was at the moment visiting his sisters on Long
Island and was telegraphed to from Chicago that
there was an important message for him from Rome.
He at once made his way back to his diocesan city,
where by this time some rumor of the promotion had
leaked out probably from Rome and confirmation
of the important news story was asked by the newspaper reporters at the archiepiscopal residence.
There they were told that there was nothing to give
out.

Archbishop Mundelein felt that the first authoritative statement of the honor about to be conferred
on him by the Pope should go not to the public
press but to his own people through the channel of
the pastors of the diocese to whom his pastoral
announcements were always addressed. This was
very typical of the man and his feelings for his
flock. He is least of all a publicity seeker. He felt
deeply, however, that his people of the archdiocese
were his children and that he should share directly
with them at the earliest possible moment the joy
there was in the direct recognition by the Father of
Christendom of their archbishop. He has declared
again and again that it was not as a matter of personal recognition that the cardinalate was offered

to him as that his great archdiocese and the million
and a half of Catholics in his flock were honored by
the Pope. This was the chief burden of the letter
which he addressed to the pastors of the diocese
to be read to their congregations on Sunday morning, after Archbishop Mundelein himself had already departed on his journey to Rome. The letter
ran:

March 7, 1924.

"REVEREND DEAR FATHER:

It is with feelings of singular joy and gratitude
that I announce to the clergy of this diocese the fact
that I have been called to Rome by Our Holy Father to be raised to the Cardinalitial dignity in the
coming Consistory on the 24th of this month. I regret that it was not possible for me to gather the
priests together before my departure to rejoice with
them and to express in person to them my appreciation of the honor that has come to me through them
and their people; but the time allowed me was too
brief and moreover the message was held confidential.

I have welcomed this signal mark of the Sovereign Pontiff's favor, because it comes not because
of any personal merit of mine but as a recognition
of the devoted loyalty of the clergy and generous
coöperation of the people of Chicago in every un-

dertaking for the glory of God and in the cause of
Christian charity and education. For that reason I
am grateful and of that I shall be mindful at the
moment of the Consistory when Pope Pius XI
raises to the Cardinalitial dignity in my humble person the first representative of the Catholicity of the
United States west of the Allegheny Mountains.

I trust that the priests of Chicago and their people may keep me in their prayers during these days,
that I may prove worthy of the honor conferred and
mindful of its responsibilities and ever a help and
consolation to the successor of St. Peter.

Sincerely yours in Christ,
GEORGE W. MUNDELEIN,
Archbishop of Chicago."

The bestowal of the cardinalate on two Americans at the same time, archbishops of the two largest Sees in America, was to open a new chapter in
the history of the relations of the papacy to the
American people. Cardinals are spoken of as
Princes of the Church and it is an index of the inheritance of the spirit of the Lord and Master Who
declared that the ultimate sign of His Church was
that "the Gospel is preached to the poor," whom we
"have always with us," that the two latest acces-
sions to the College of Cardinals should both have

come as the result of the papal desire to afford due recognition to America for all that her people had done for the poor of Europe in their time of need. The Pope wanted to emphasize the fact that the reason for the appointment of two American cardinals at the same time was that the American people had demonstrated by their readiness to help the distressed of all nations in the trying disturbed period after the war, a spirit of beneficence which deserved the highest recognition that the Church could give. The keynote of the proceedings was struck in this and it resounded all through the various parts of the ceremony by which the two American archbishops were inducted into the cardinalate.

Some idea of the deep feeling of affection and grateful reverence for the charity of the people of the United States that touched the heart of Pope Pius XI for all the beneficence which they had exercised during the war and after it for the distressed people of Europe, can be gathered from the address which he made on the occasion of the official creation of the two American cardinals. This address (called an allocution) was delivered at the Consistory of all the cardinals held in the Vatican March 24, 1924, when the Pope proclaimed the new cardinals. He said, "In the immense family which God has confided to us, there are brothers more favored by Divine Providence, who through the Father of All come to the assistance of their less fortunate brothers in their trials and disasters. Our heart is touched, and at the same time exalted toward God, thinking of and beholding their magnificent acts of filial piety and fraternal charity. We find pleasure in expressing to them from this exalted place, in this distinguished assembly, a fervent declaration of our gratitude, that of a father who feels himself much indebted on behalf of his suffering children.

"As soon as we had lifted our voice to ask for help for the starving children of Russia, the episcopacy, clergy and people of the United States answered with promptness, enthusiasm and generosity which placed them, and ever since has maintained them, in the front rank of this new crusade of charity. We feel, however, that something would be wanting in this expression of gratitude if special mention were not made of the position and part which the United States of America took and maintained in this concourse of charity. This beneficence, shown everywhere and by all, continued for a long time; we can say that it even still continues, though gradually reduced in proportion as the days advanced in which the need diminished.

"Later we intimated that fresh miseries and necessities had arisen in various parts of the world.

It was only an intimation, as, indeed, discretion counseled, but it was sufficient to enkindle again everywhere fresh ardor to bestow money and material according to the varying possibilities. The slight intimation was sufficient to move the hierarchy, clergy and people, not only to maintain their primacy, but to push forward and upward, so they are seen to excel even the grand and wonderful deeds of charity they had previously performed.

"It being an impossibility to express in words all that our heart feels at this historical and epic wave of charity, we have decided to express ourselves with a gesture which, touching as it does the very summit of the sacred hierarchy, shall be visible to all, and in its mute eloquence shall convey our thought, first of all to that great and most noble people and country, which in such a glorious task has been able to conquer such an enviable primacy."

And then came this happy culmination:

"We have thought of raising to the honor of the sacred purple and of your Sacred College two prelates who, for their personal qualities, for their zeal, for the importance of their Sees and for the merits of their pastoral ministry are honored in the ecclesiastical hierarchy in the United States. If this action is extraordinary, the reasons which inspire it are without parallel, and no less extraordinary."

The expressions used by the Pope with regard to America had been so full of love and admiration for this country that the Consistory in which he used them has been spoken of as "the American Consistory." Two days later when the cardinals were present in the Vatican on March 26th, for the imposition of the red birettas Cardinal Mundelein as the senior of the two cardinals in the hierarchy made the response for both and thanked the Pope particularly in the name of all Americans for the kindly words of appreciation which he had spoken. That address, brief though it is, is of great historical import, because it relates to that characteristic American trait of helpfulness for all suffering people which was manifested so supremely by the Americans in dealing with needy nations since the war. Cardinal Mundelein said, "From the distant shores first discovered by the great Genoese we have come at your call to receive from your venerable hands the most exalted dignity the Holy Church can give her sons. Fully aware of our own littleness, and not without fear and trepidation, we have come to the feet of your Holiness, but we are heartened by the same goodness that is reached out to us, that kindness which in these troublesome times of public calamities resulting from the World War has made his Holiness a Good Samaritan to suffering humanity, a providential Pontiff of charity, modeled after the Divine Master, who went about doing good."

Pope Piux XI took occasion in responding to the address of Cardinal Mundelein to express his supreme admiration for America and at the same time to emphasize his appreciation of all that America had done, was doing and surely would continue to do for the benefit of the rest of the civilized world. It was this portion of the ceremonies which brought out the expression of the Pope's feelings as the Father of Christendom that deeply impressed all those who were present. The feelings of one of the witnesses, himself probably the greatest of living historians, certainly the historical writer whose knowledge of the history of Rome made him most appropriately responsive, we shall quote in his own words after giving the brief address of the Pope which called them forth.

"Our most happy and affectionate welcome to you, most beloved sons, who come from that great land, America. Twice welcome, because as citizens and shepherds of that great country you came to this our Rome, which is also yours; because you are our sons, priests of the Holy Roman Church. This great love of your youth, this great light that preceded and has presided over your ecclesiastical development renders more splendid in force and splendor of radiation these words, 'Priests of the Holy Roman Church.'

"Welcome to you, who come to let us hear beautiful things; high, consoling things, such as you have just spoken! Truly, we have heard of the great faith of your people, of the magnificent development of their Christian life, of their flaming devotion to the Holy Faith and the Holy See, to the Vicar of Jesus Christ and to the Eucharistic Jesus himself.

"All this fills us with purest joy and gives us the golden key to the magnificent mystery of the miracles of charity which your country has shown us. All this convinces us that we have been well inspired in seeking and finding a means to demonstrate to your great people all our gratitude, all our paternal pleasure in honoring that people in your persons with the sacred Roman purple.

"You are not only representatives of that people, luminous representatives, but also specifically the representatives of that episcopate and clergy who in preparing that miracle of charity, as in the development of a magnificent Christian life, allowed it to be said of them: 'As are the priests, so are the people.'"

And then the Pope proceeded with solemn words that are both history and prophecy:

"The drama of sorrow and charity is unending;

it lasts as long as the world. Just so unending is the drama of divine pity. This great drama seldom has such a large and potent life as in your country. Life in the United States a century ago could be summed up in the small space of a few numbers. What has it not become in so short a time? Speaking only of what we have seen, America's intervention decided the fate of Europe and the world. To-day its charity saves from hunger and death millions of individuals. What will it be in fifty years, in another century? If life continues to throb as now, what will the country be able to give, on which the Divine hand has bestowed such treasures, where men's hearts contain measures of intelligence and force, immensely more precious?"

It is very interesting, as we have said, to note how these ceremonies in Rome struck a great modern mind whose familiarity with the history of the past affords him a background on which the events of to-day can be seen in a perspective that gives them something of their place for all time.

Guglielmo Ferrero, who must probably be considered as the leading living historian of Europe in our day, was present at the Consistory in which the new cardinals were created. He confessed that he had probably never been so thrilled at any ceremony as at this and his description of what he saw is one of the classics of such literature. He was the representative of a number of American papers and his account appeared in many parts of the country. After describing the approach of Archbishop Mundelein who as senior in the episcopate was the first to advance to the foot of the throne of His Holiness who placed on his shoulders the mozetta and on his head the red biretta and then of the same ceremony for Archbishop Hayes, he records the fact that Cardinal Mundelein thanked His Holiness for the great honor of the purple which he had bestowed on him. And then he adds:

"What the Archbishop said and what the Pope said you know from the official reports, but there is something which no reading of just the text of the two speeches can convey. It is the sense of fatherly, loving kindness which the Pope's words infuse into our hearts; fatherly, loving kindness which seemed to spread itself over us as we listened and from us spread itself, like the widening ripples over the surface of a pond into which a stone has been cast, over Italy, over all Europe, over all America." The great historian deeply touched proceeded:

"With my eyes fixed on him and listening with rapt attention as he spoke, it came home to me that I was feeling nothing in the least resembling what I had felt in the presence of other authorities, those of the earth. They represent the force and the rude justice of man keeping as best they can by the power of menace and of the sword a certain order in the world.

"But as the words issued from the lips of the Pope there grew on me the realization of what he had expressed in the secret Consistory with the words, 'the universal fatherhood entrusted by God to his vicar on earth.'

"It was a sweet and deeply restful feeling of a rising in the heart of consolation and of hope. Every time that, since the war, I have spoken with one of those who have power on earth, I have come away more troubled than ever over the future in store for us.

"When one speaks with these all seems egotism, bitterness, pride, obstinacy, lack of humanity—the spirit of the times. To-day, no. Listening to-day it seemed to me that at last Europe had recognized and praised in words of beauty and of deep paternal love, issuing in Rome from the lips of her oldest and most august authority, all that America had done to relieve the sufferings of the world." The Roman historian's soul was lifted to prophecy:

"As I heard the solemn 'Thank you' of the Pope spoken to America in the name not only of the Church but of all generous souls in the Old World, I felt that the powers of good, engaged though they be in fierce war with the power of evil, have not yet been and never will be overcome."

The ceremony ended, the United States had two additional cardinals, who returned to the United States clothed with their new dignity and their new powers to go on with their organization of the work of Christianity for the benefit of their countrymen. The welcome which they received on their return is the index of how much the people of the United States and especially of those who knew them the best appreciated the honor which had been conferred on them.   Both cardinals came back with their hearts full of zeal and renewed purpose to devote themselves to the interests of their people, their country and of Christianity.

The welcome accorded in Chicago partaking as might well be expected of the generous open-heartedness of the West and especially of the enthusiasm of the citizens of what they like to call their "breezy city," was a celebration never to be forgotten by those who witnessed it.   It represented one of the greatest outbursts of enthusiastic good feeling that had ever been seen in this country.   Only great patriotic celebrations on special occasions have ever equaled it and probably not even these have ever surpassed it.   The Chicago people of all classes and creeds took to their hearts their first cardinal and made him feel that he had indeed become one of them and that they were proud to greet him, feeling that the honors conferred on him were reflected on them. Some of the scenes of that celebration almost beggar description in the enthusiasm that was evoked and even the fluent pens of Chicago journalists found it difficult to describe in any adequate way the manifestations of feeling that had been evoked among the people.

Cardinal Mundelein's first thought after the celebration of welcome was over was of the organization of a great session of the International Eucharistic Congress to be held in Chicago in the latter part of June, 1926. The preparations for that indicate clearly what a tremendously significant event it will be for stirring up faith in the Christ of the Last Supper and the Eucharistic memorial of Himself that He left. The seminary grounds out at St. Mary's of the Lake will form a magnificent setting for the procession and afford a charmingly beautiful background for certain Church ceremonies in connection with the Congress. The cardinal has devoted himself to the organization of this on a grand scale and with his well-known powers of organization there is no doubt at all that Chicago will witness in this, the twenty-eighth Congress to be held, the greatest session of the Eucharistic Congress that has ever assembled and that American Catholics will give an unforgettable demonstration of their profound reverence for their Eucharistic Lord.

PATRICK, CARDINAL HAYES

CARDINAL HAYES was born in New York City down in that lower part of Manhattan now known as the lower East Side where besides himself within a few blocks and within a few years of each other Cardinal Mundelein and Governor Alfred E. Smith of New York were also born. His birthday was November 20, 1867. His parents, Daniel and Mary Gleeson, lived in City Hall Place close by St. Andrew's Church. The future cardinal archbishop of New York was born not only in the shadow of the historic old church but also in the shadow of the City Hall. He was a typical New York boy and has lived the life of New York consciously for well above fifty years now and knows the history of his native city as few others know it. As might almost be expected under the circumstances, he is a great "booster" for New York, and thinks that many people for political and other reasons are prone to misrepresent the metropolis or to smirch its fair name. There is nothing that he resents more than any tendency to make our greatest American city appear in a more unfavorable light than it deserves.

His mother died when he was but little more than an infant and for some years he remained in the care of his father who sent him to the parish school of the neighboring Church of the Transfiguration because there was at that time no Catholic school in St. Andrew's parish. While he was still but a mere boy he went to live with his mother's sister, Mrs. James Egan, who with her husband resided in Madison Street. This brought the future archbishop into St. James' parish so that from personal experience he knows the early conditions and the history of Catholicity in down-town Manhattan very well. His uncle and aunt lavished all the care on him they could possibly have given him if he were their own son and as they were devoutly Catholic, intensely devoted to their religion, they exercised the greatest solicitude to have their nephew guarded from the many moral dangers which so constantly threaten the children of a great city in their free intercourse with other children on the streets.

Their fostering care was rewarded to the full. Mrs. Egan lived to see her nephew and adopted son ordained a priest and later had the supreme happi-

G. Folici

CARDINAL HAYES

ness and privilege of seeing him consecrated auxiliary bishop and of knowing that he was chosen archbishop of the diocese. She died two years too soon to have the supreme pleasure, as it would have been to her, of knowing that he was chosen as cardinal and of seeing him come back to New York clothed with the new dignity. His uncle however, Mr. James Egan, lived to enjoy that pleasure and was among the group of enthusiastic old friends who greeted his nephew affectionately at Quarantine on his return from Rome after having been accorded the distinction of Prince of the Church. The cardinal's greeting in return as all who saw it noted well was that of a son.

While living in Madison Street with the Egans, young Patrick Hayes was so successful at school and displayed such talent that his uncle and aunt were tempted to make the sacrifice—no small one for them—of sending him to the old De La Salle Institute in Second Street conducted by the Christian Brothers. From here he was graduated at the completion of what would now be called high-school studies in 1886. Owing to his wish to go on with his education his uncle and aunt now sent him to Manhattan College then situated at 133rd Street and Broadway to continue his studies. Already the desire was uppermost in his mind to become a priest and Manhattan College was the great nursery for New York priests at that time. Besides priests however a great many of the men who afterwards became prominent in the Catholic life of New York were educated there.

The old buildings are still standing as this is written and they constitute a never ending source of wonder as to how the good Brothers of the Christian Schools ever succeeded in accommodating in them in those last decades of the nineteenth century the large group of earnest students who have succeeded so admirably in every walk of life in "little old New York" in the years ever since. How under the crowded conditions that must have existed they succeeded in giving their students a genuine education that quite literally brought out their powers of mind must always remain a mystery. Men who were distinguished in medicine, at the bar, above all in the judiciary as well as in the Church, went through old Manhattan under the rather straitened circumstances of those old days and appear to have gotten more out of their educational opportunities, such as they were, than modern schools seem able to give. Now when elaborate educational equipment seems to be so all important as to be almost indispensable it is interesting to note the results secured in the very limited facilities of an old-fashioned college. Mark Hopkins at one end of a log and a student at the other may make a university. It is what is brought out of the student, not what is poured in, that counts, and old Manhattan's education measured well up to standard in that regard.

The future cardinal graduated at Manhattan College in 1888, and began his theological studies at St. Joseph's Seminary, Troy, N. Y., in September of that year. He succeeded admirably in his studies but was noted above all for his thoroughly religious spirit, his perfect accord with the discipline of the house and the friendships which his goodness of heart and cheerful happy ways made for him. He was so well thought of that he was ordained priest on September 8, 1892, some months ahead of his class and then was given the privilege of special theological studies at the Catholic University of America in Washington. He is one of the first significant fruits of that great university, an index of its power to train minds for higher things, that has meant so much for the Church in this country.

At the end of his second year of studies at the Catholic University in June, 1894, the young priest was appointed assistant or curate at St. Gabriel's Church on East 37th Street, New York, where his predecessor in the archiepiscopate, the late Cardinal

Farley, was then the rector, filling at the same time the duties of the office of vicar general of the diocese. Monsignor Farley had at this time been for nearly ten years the pastor of St. Gabriel's and was looked up to as one of the most prominent priests of the archdiocese. The two future cardinals were thus brought intimately in touch with each other and the older man came to appreciate the younger one very highly.

It was not surprising then that when Monsignor Farley was consecrated auxiliary bishop of New York he chose Father Hayes who had been his assistant for some five years as his secretary. Seven years later, in 1902, when Bishop Farley was nominated to the archbishopric the young priest went with him as his secretary and it was very evident that further preferment in the Church would almost inevitably come to him. It was not long before Father Hayes was appointed the Chancellor of the archdiocese and filled this very responsible position with its many details of administration so admirably that when the question of the appointment of an auxiliary bishop came up his name very naturally was suggested for it by Archbishop Farley, and accepted at Rome. In the meantime Father Hayes' achievement in the organization of the Cathedral College had made it very clear that here was a man whose administrative abilities could be absolutely depended on for important work requiring the exercise of tact, and a knowledge of men, as well as intellectual ability.

In the meantime honors from Rome began to come to him. In 1903 the year of his appointment as Chancellor of the Archdiocese and of his organization of Cathedral College he received his first official recognition from Rome in the form of the degree of Doctor of Divinity. Four years later in 1907 Rev. Dr. Hayes was appointed domestic prelate by His Holiness Pope Pius X with the title of Monsignor. Seven years later Monsignor Hayes while in Rome with Cardinal Farley was appointed Auxiliary Bishop of New York on June 1, 1914, by Pope Pius X whose death as the result of the shock of the awful war that had broken out was to come only a few months later. Each of these positions imposed new and special duties and Dr. Hayes proved not only equal to them but demonstrated a power of control over details which showed very clearly his own strength of personality and his ability to understand men and see the deeper meaning of questions behind details that came to him. In the midst of all he won and held the friendship, cordial and enduring, of all those with whom he was brought in contact and especially in whose regard he had to fulfill the duties of the various offices which he held.

As Chancellor of the Archdiocese of New York Monsignor Hayes had to keep in touch with not only every church but every clergyman in the diocese. There were many hundreds of churches and still more hundreds of clergymen but so thoroughly did he accomplish this work which came to him that it was often said that he knew all the priests in the diocese not only by name but in the intimate personal way that enabled him to understand their problems sometimes almost better than they did themselves. He knew their histories, knew what they were doing for their parishes and what they were planning to do, was well aware how they were fulfilling their priestly duties and recognized the zeal they had for the Church. If these duties as chancellor were all he had to do perhaps the task would not have seemed so great, but he was besides the secretary of the archbishop and the president of Cathedral College and these duties added detail upon detail of responsibility that must have occupied every moment of the day and might very well be expected at times to invade some of the night.

Even all this however does not complete the tale of his duties. He was a contributor of important articles to the *Catholic Encyclopedia* as well as to the Catholic University *Bulletin*. He wrote for the *North American Review* an interpretation of the new marriage law, *Ne temere* (so called because of the initial Latin words in the papal decree promulgating it) which was an admirable piece of work for its clearness, accuracy and brevity. Such an article was needed very much at that time because there had been rather serious misunderstandings with regard to the new Roman Catholic marriage law. It had been said, though of course quite without reason, that the Church absolutely refused to recognize the validity of marriages contracted without the Church's blessing. This was not true except for members of the Church thoroughly aware of the Church's legislation in the matter. This legislation was for Catholics and not for those outside of the Church. The Sacrament of Marriage has for its ministers the wedded couple themselves and not the clergyman who performs the ceremony. Monsignor Hayes brought out very well the distinctions in this matter and made it very clear just what the Church legislation aimed at accomplishing in order to make matrimony more sacred and solemn than the tendency of the modern world was prone to permit it to be.

It was undoubtedly his work at the Cathedral College which first called particular attention to

Father Hayes's power as an executive and an administrator. The Cathedral College is a preparatory seminary which affords high-school and college training for youths who feel that they may have a vocation to the priesthood. The object of the "little seminary" as it is called throughout the Catholic world is to give to aspirants for the priesthood a broad foundation of education devoting special attention in the course of it to what concerns their future vocation to the Catholic ministry. The policy of the Church has always been to take boys in their impressionable younger years from twelve to fourteen and provide them with a solid fundamental education which at the same time includes a special training of heart and mind in religious matters.

It is well understood that a certain percentage of the boys who in their early teens think they have a vocation to the priesthood will prove after a time not to be suited for the life or will develop ambitions along other lines. It is important then to give them such an education as will prove useful for a career in the world and the idea of thoroughness of education for any and every purpose as a solid foundation for future work in any line must be the policy of the preparatory seminary if it is to be successful. The organization of such an institution then requires rather nice adjustment of educational details and above all demands special regulation of the educational forces that make for training of character. Nowhere should the maxim of President Hibben of Princeton be better exemplified as the keynote of education than in the little seminary. "Let us make men and they will find their work." That I know was the idea that was uppermost in the mind of Rev. Dr. Hayes in the early days of the founding of Cathedral College.

Cardinal Farley committed the organization of the new institution to Father Hayes with perfect confidence though this quiet young man had not deeply impressed himself upon many people. The result was most interesting. It goes almost without saying that the number of students in such an institution in a great Catholic archdiocese like New York City would grow very rapidly. Actually in the course of half a dozen of years there were some five hundred students in attendance. Any one who thinks that candidates for the priesthood in the Roman Catholic Church are few in proportion to the needs or are decreasing in recent years because of modernistic tendencies should take the opportunity sometime to study the statistics of the various seminaries little and grand as they are called that have been founded throughout the country. Those of the Cathedral College are particularly interesting

in this regard. It is easy to understand however
that with such a rapid growth without definite traditions to guide both masters and pupils, abuses may
readily creep in. It is not easy to foresee needs
and details of policy and it is hard to regulate the
various phases of college activity and yet encourage
their development while at the same time co-
ordinating the elements of the curriculum.

From very early in the organization of the college I was among those asked to serve on the
faculty. I have continued my connection with it as
professor of physiological psychology for nearly
twenty years. It was a never ending source of surprise to me to note how smoothly everything worked
in the early days of the developmental period of
Cathedral College. New machinery is likely to
creak some and to knock occasionally and then there
is an injunction about not running it too fast until a
considerable amount of mileage has been covered
so that the various portions of the machinery groove
themselves into coördination with all the others.
The growth of the college students in number at the
Cathedral College together with the high-school
students necessitated the educational machine going
rather rapidly and yet everything ran along so
smoothly as to be quite satisfactory. Indeed the
college seemed almost to run of itself. I need

scarcely say however that any one familiar with institutions that bring together any considerable number of human beings and especially youthful human beings from twelve to eighteen is not likely to think that they run of themselves. When they go smoothly and get over ground well, some place there is a master hand guiding them and directing them to good purposes. When they are successful, the guiding is probably not from without but there is a definite and successful appeal to great motives within the human beings most concerned which serves to keep them on the straight path without straining.

When the college curriculum was completed and the classes were filled up to the Senior year, the Board of Regents of New York State was asked to examine the school for the purpose of rating it as to the conferring of degrees and this examination proved to be scarcely more than a formality since the college had been so well organized that it was easy to appreciate its right to the Regents' recognition.

It was perfectly clear after this that the young chancellor of the archdiocese so quiet and unassuming in his ways, so cheerful in his relations with all those with whom he was brought in contact, so ready to see the humor of things while intent on accomplishing all that was best, would go far in the ad-

ministrative life of the Church for the organization
of the Cathedral College afforded rather striking
evidence of his ability to do work in that friction-
less way that is so important to assure success in
Church movements and religious purposes. *Ohne
Hast, ohne Rast,* is the motto of religious movement—"without haste and without waste movement."

With the war came the necessity for the organization of chaplains for the Army and very soon it
came to be realized that that army would amount to
several millions of men and that though the Catholic percentage in the nation is only about 20 per cent,
the number of Catholics among the soldiers and
sailors of the Army and Navy was nearly 40 per
cent. Here was an immense task of organization to
be accomplished. There were a great many volunteers to do chaplain work both in the camps here and
in the camps abroad, with ever so many younger
and not a few older men clamoring for the opportunity to work among the men at the front in spite
of the danger to life and limb that might be involved. It was important to select those who would
be most valuable for the purpose and then to see
that they obtained such training as would enhance
their value and make them of the greatest possible
service to the Army. Here was a job that was big

enough for man-sized shoulders indeed and it seemed as if it might be too large for any one man. When Rome was questioned with regard to it the Papal Secretary of State suggested that as New York was the principal port of debarkation for the troops and as Bishop Hayes was the auxiliary bishop of New York he was the logical man for the position and the ecclesiastical authorities felt that they could entrust this immense responsibility to him without any hesitation as to what the results would surely be in order and efficiency.

Accordingly, on November 29, 1917, Bishop Hayes was appointed by the Holy See to be Bishop Ordinary of the Armed Forces of the United States. When the number of chaplains multiplied so as to be commensurate with the large numbers of the men enlisted, it very soon became clear that they could not remain under the jurisdiction of their respective bishops or archbishops scattered throughout the country, but that there would have to be some central authority directly connected with the military department. Hence the appointment of Bishop Hayes to that position which almost needless to say carried with it an immense responsibility. In his episcopal capacity as bishop of the forces he supervised the work of the Catholic chaplains in the Army and Navy and had to make episcopal visitations of

a great many of the camps in this country during
the war. War conditions had a tendency to relax
the ordinary discipline of the priesthood and circumstances tended to do away with many of the
safeguards that hedged the lives of young priests
particularly in their work in the ordinary service of
the Church. All this added to the responsibility
that was placed on the shoulders of Bishop Hayes
and his response to that was of itself a fine demonstration of his personal character and administrative
ability.

A great many chaplains were needed for the literally millions of soldiers who were enlisted during
the war, for though the United States participated
in the war operations for only a little more than a
year, over two million of men were under arms.
As Military Bishop of the United States, through
the ready coöperation of the American hierarchy,
Bishop Hayes secured some nine hundred priests to
serve as chaplains, commissioned and non-commis-
sioned, both here and in Europe. By a very unusual
extension of jurisdiction necessitated by war conditions, his diocese was not only commensurate with
the whole United States but also included every portion of the world where there were American Catholic chaplains or soldiers or sailors in the service of
the United States government. This was a task

indeed but it was fulfilled admirably and Bishop Hayes' success in it undoubtedly constituted one of the important reasons why after the death of his Archbishop, Cardinal Farley, in September, 1918, he was selected to succeed him as Archbishop of New York.

How he accomplished that task can be best told in the words of the oldest of navy chaplains who for twenty-five years has been occupied with naval duties and who if any one was able to estimate how much Cardinal Hayes as camp bishop accomplished for the fighting forces of the United States Army and Navy in the World War. Rev. Matthew C. Gleeson, U.S.N., in his address delivered on behalf of the Army and Navy on the occasion of the solemn reception of His Eminence, Patrick, Cardinal Hayes, at St. Patrick's Cathedral, New York, April 30, 1924, said, "Under ordinary circumstances the tributes offered by your priests and people would have been adequate to the demands of the occasion, but in the case of Your Eminence, associations of national significance seemed to insist that you be welcomed not only as the Cardinal Archbishop of New York, but as the Chaplain Bishop of the Army and Navy.

"For, aside from the dignity that is yours as Met-tropolitan, you have spiritual ties which bind you to the nation itself, and commission you to authority in every land and on every sea where the flag of our country keeps watch and ward. Not alone are you head of the greatest archdiocese in Christendom, next to St. Peter's own, but you are the spiritual leader of the forces of national defense, and as such, have under your supervision every priest, and every layman of the faith, who is privileged to wear its uniform. When it came then to give place to those who had official claim upon this unique opportunity, it was deemed fitting that the clergy and the laity of the United Services should have the distinction of extending to you a special welcome of their own.

"And in this message of greeting and of congratulation, Your Eminence, along with those now on active duty is associated every priest and every religious who had the honor of serving under you during the World War. You are our first Military Bishop. You came to us in the crisis of a great emergency, and to you as *Ordinarius Castrensis* was committed the herculean task of providing at short notice the Catholic Chaplain quota, necessary to cope with the need of our armies. In the pursuit of this duty, it was yours to select from a legion of volunteers the priests best fitted in youth and in strength for active service; to provide them with everything essential to the ministry of their sacred office, and to build up the machinery of an Ordinariate, capable of meeting at every angle the call of spiritual ministration, both afloat and ashore. Single-handed, it might be said, and without a precedent to follow, you prosecuted this undertaking with apostolic zeal and fervent patriotism. You spared no personal sacrifice, recognized neither difficulty nor trouble, communicated your own enthusiasm to all with whom you came in contact, with the result that long before our armed forces were ready for action, you had your chaplains commissioned, equipped, and in the field. The success which rewarded your efforts is now a matter of historic record. It earned for Your Eminence the thanks of a grateful nation. It won for you the abiding gratitude of your Catholic fellow citizens. It made your name a benediction at home and abroad; and those of us who were with you in the comradeship it forged are proud to feel that it was the one achievement which put the supreme *cachet* upon your genius as an administrator, shaped your whole after career as a prelate, made you an outstanding figure in an illustrious hierarchy, and helped to render inevitable the splendid consummation of attainment, which we glory in this morning."

Besides his work as Bishop of the United States Armed Forces, Bishop Hayes took an active part in every patriotic undertaking that was organized for the help of soldiers and sailors, or calculated in any way to win the War. He was one of the four bishops chosen to constitute the executive committee of the Catholic War Council. This Council was composed of the members of the American hierarchy which by fortunate coincidence found itself in session in Baltimore at the time of the declaration of war and immediately offered every possible service to the country through the hands of President Wilson who appreciated very deeply their enthusiastic patriotism and expressed his sense of personal obligation for their hearty good wishes and good will. In order that the hierarchy might constantly be in a position to exercise its influence, the executive committee of the Catholic War Council met frequently and to them was referred most of the questions that came up during the war as regards the fulfillment of the promise of the hierarchy and the affording of the most complete coöperation to the government.

Bishop Hayes under Cardinal Farley's direction was constantly occupied with war work of one kind or another. He was the inspiration and the director of the Knights of Columbus drive for war

funds which realized nearly five million dollars and
which initiated the Knights of Columbus war activities that were to prove so heartening to the soldiers
both at the camps in this country and in the field
operations abroad. Without "Casey" in France
one of the picturesque activities of the war would
have been lacking and many a young soldier would
have missed the stimulus to his morale that came
from contact with them. A little later during the
war Bishop Hayes was one of the directors of the
United War Work drive which secured for distribution to the various social agencies attached to
the camps and to the troops in the field over $170,-
000,000. In the course of these drives Bishop
Hayes made many addresses and what he had to
say, brief and to the point, coming from a man
who himself was devoting all his efforts for the
benefit of the soldiers and sailors proved very effective. His words were a source of inspiration
that brought a great many people to make further
sacrifices for the winning of the war.

On March 10, 1919, Pope Benedict XV, ap-
pointed Bishop Hayes to succeed Cardinal Farley
as archbishop of New York. On March 19, St.
Joseph's day, the new archbishop was installed in
St. Patrick's Cathedral by the Most Reverend John
Bonzano, apostolic delegate and personal represen-

tative of the pope in such matters in this country. The occasion was notable and was attended by an immense crowd of people who filled the cathedral and all the surrounding streets. There were addresses on behalf of the clergy by Right Reverend Monsignor Mooney who had been for many years the Vicar General of the New York archdiocese and a dear personal friend of Bishop Hayes; on behalf of the army and navy chaplains by Monsignor Waring who had occupied a position in relation to the chaplains under Bishop Hayes' authority resembling that of the Vicar General of a diocese. Finally there was an address given on behalf of the laity by Justice Victor J. Dowling of the appellate division of the Supreme Court of the State of New York. The people of the archdiocese were pleased beyond measure that the appointment had come to one whose many years of service in the archdiocese made it clear beyond all doubt that the policy of his predecessors which had accomplished so much for Catholicity in New York was to be continued.

Just five years later on March 24, 1924, Pope Pius XI created Archbishop Hayes of New York and Archbishop Mundelein of Chicago, cardinals. Both had had excellent success in organizing the religious activities of their archdioceses. Cardinal

Hayes's reorganization of the charities of New York had demonstrated his administrative ability in large affairs and the call to the cardinalate was not unexpected except perhaps by the future cardinal himself. New York proceeded to exhibit its pride over the fact that a New York boy out of the heart of old New York had reached the dignity of cardinal. The receptions on his return from Rome on the part of all manner of people of his own flock and of those not of it must have touched his heart deeply and made him realize how thoroughly he was appreciated by his own folk.

Cardinal Hayes's feelings toward New York were very well demonstrated by the message which he sent from his steamer on the way back just as soon as he was able to get in touch by wireless with his native city. That message was very characteristic. It was, "God bless little old New York." As has been said the "little old New Yorkers" knew what he meant. He was undoubtedly homesick for the old town. He had had enough of the pomp and circumstance of old Rome and now he was hungry to get back to "little old New York." He wanted to know just how the city would react to the fact that a boy born down on the lower East Side was come back to be its cardinal archbishop. New York had a warm place in his heart and he wanted to find how warm was the place that he occupied in the heart of New York. Almost needless to say he was destined to be completely satisfied in that matter just as soon as he landed but in the meantime there were days to wait and though steamers might be fast they were not fast enough for one heart at least that was separated from its own and longed to be back among the old town folks.

In the banquet given him after his arrival in this country by the Catholic Club at the Waldorf-Astoria before more than fifteen hundred laymen including a large number of distinguished non-Catholic citizens of New York, Cardinal Hayes said, "Let no one fear that the making of the Archbishop of New York a Cardinal has made him less an American." And then he added in terms that might very well have come from that other great American cardinal, Archbishop Gibbons, "One thing comes to me at this hour—I feel that America will always be right. America is bound to grow and prosper, she is bound to broaden, she is bound to fulfill a mission that Divine Providence has set for her—she is bound to do it when men like you will come and pay tribute to a shepherd. For you are here to pay tribute to a cardinal shepherd. There have been cardinal statesmen, there have been cardinal scholars, there have been cardinal scientists, but I am here to-night only as a cardinal shepherd."

Cardinal Hayes likes to talk of himself as the shepherd of his flock. He has said over and over again in public addresses that he does not like people to think of him so much as a cardinal or archbishop, as of a shepherd. The tenderness in his heart is well-known. He has a gentleness and a fatherly solicitude for those with whom he comes in contact that has made him deeply beloved by all those who know him well but that has given him a very warm place in the hearts of those who are brought in contact with him even but transitorily. He is a man whose heart is developed even more than his head, though he was looked upon as one of the most talented of students in his school days. That sum of kindly feeling for mankind which has been suggested as the definition of what is meant by the "heart" is surely developed in him to a notable degree.

The result is that his influence is not confined or limited to those of the Catholic faith though as head of the New York archdiocese Cardinal Hayes is the spiritual leader of nearly 1,500,000 devoted Catholics. In addition to these an increasing number of non-Catholics are constantly seeking him and above all looking to his decisions and pronouncements for direction in the difficult social problems that our generation presents. The cardinal's fearless stand on religious questions and his simple definite expression of faith when contrasted with the doubt and hesitancy as to essentials to be noted in public expressions of some of the leaders of non-Catholic creeds, has prompted a great many of those not directly of the cardinal's flock to seek his advice. It has been said that he knows New York, root and branch, but he also knows New Yorkers very well and New Yorkers know him and trust him. There is no doubt at all that his occupation of the position of archbishop of New York will redound greatly to the benefit of the archdiocese and of the Catholic Church in this country but also that it will have a very definite effect for good on the life of the American people and the social and religious conditions of our country.

The appointment of these two cardinals, archbishops of Chicago and New York, was entirely due to the pope's wish to make public recognition of the gratitude that he felt that Europe and the Church owed to the Americans for all that they had accomplished to save the suffering peoples of Europe from starvation just after the World War when things were in such bad condition. Cardinal Hayes said of the address of the pope on the occasion of the conferment of these honors upon Americans that it was very evident that His Holiness had been deeply touched by all that he knew America had accomplished and that his one desire was to make Americans feel that all their goodness had been deeply appreciated. Cardinal Hayes said, "I know that I am welcomed home, first of all, as an American citizen who has been honored by the most ancient and venerable spiritual throne in the world. Pope Pius XI in every utterance made it quite clear that his desire was to honor America, not for any political, scientific or economic achievement; not for any advantage there might accrue to the Catholic Church in America; not to gain favor with the American people, but because of American charity to suffering humanity. America's Catholicity of charity dispensing to the ends of the earth, a largess of mercy, hope and courage with the necessaries of life has gained for our glorious republic a prestige and a position among nations which none can take from her—and a benediction from heaven which will serve our beloved land in these critical hours of the world's history."

On his arrival in this country Cardinal Hayes had emphasized the fact that the papal consistory in which the two American cardinals had been created had been all American in its proceedings. He said, "One of the vivid impressions that I carried away from there was that the ceremony was so entirely American. The two Cardinals who were created were Americans. The Holy Father made repeated references to America, and this, together with the number of Americans in Rome, conveyed to all the general impression that it was an American Consistory."

Of the many duties that his great archdiocese, which contains more practical Catholics than any other diocese in the world, imposes on him, the work that Archbishop Hayes has taken most to heart has been the establishment on a broad firm basis of the charities of the archdiocese. Deep down in his heart there is the profound conviction that the greatest of Christian virtues is charity and that the fulfillment of the second of the two Commandments in which the Lord Himself summed up the whole law and the prophets, "Thou shalt love thy neighbor as thyself," is the supreme index of Christian living. With this in mind just as soon as he became archbishop of New York, he proceeded to work out a solution of the problems of charity that are necessarily so many in his large archdiocese. Ever since his heart has been in the work of doing more and more for charity, relieving suffering, preventing penury and want, helping those who need help but above all helping people to help themselves and he has been a source of inspiration for all his archdiocese to devote themselves to the work of charity. He himself has done more than any one else and his constant interest has kept others at work until now what has been accomplished has become a model for the other dioceses in the Catholic world, an outstanding example of the immense amount of good that can be accomplished by proper coördination of charitable work.

The first step in this important matter was taken when his Eminence, Cardinal Farley, in the fall of 1913, organized the United Catholic Works, a movement very necessary at that time for the need of reorganization of Catholic charities was very much felt. Under his guidance this new departure made an excellent beginning and seemed certain of producing the most beneficial results. The war years which followed until the end of 1918 disturbed conditions to such an extent that Cardinal Farley's plan for the development of the United Catholic Works was not carried through to the full realization that he had hoped and confidently looked for. As the Auxiliary Bishop of New York Cardinal Hayes had been very much interested in this project and appreciated very thoroughly how much of benefit would surely accrue from it. He had given him-

self whole-heartedly to the new development because he felt that nothing could be of so much help
not only for the poor themselves but for the proper
understanding of Christianity by those outside of
the Church.

Immediately after his appointment as archbishop
at the annual diocesan retreat in June, 1919, he an-
nounced to the assembled priests of the archdiocese
his purpose of charity reorganization. He outlined
some of his plans but declared that he felt that the
most important initial step was to learn about the
needs of Catholic charities in the archdiocese by
having a careful and thorough survey of the charity
situation made. His Grace called a meeting of
some four hundred people, representative of the religious orders and laity, who were in charge of various Catholic works throughout the archdiocese.
They were invited to coöperate in presenting details
of information. A separate report was submitted
for every institution, agency and parish studied in
their relations to charity. Some of these reports
went into several hundred pages. Public officials as
well as representatives of private agencies of various kinds were visited and consulted and their opin-
ions particularly with regard to Catholic charitable
works were obtained. The survey took over six
months to complete, but it brought out everything

of interest and importance in the matter of Catholic charities, so that a commencement might be made on a firm basis of as nearly complete knowledge as possible. This study brought to light the vast number and great variety of Catholic charitable activities in the diocese and showed there was scarcely an avenue of charity but that had been opened up by the Church in the diocese—orphanages, hospitals, boys' and girls' clubs, settlement houses, nurseries, working girls' homes, convalescent homes, fresh-air camps and other activities, all working effectively, yet quietly, without the Catholic people ever realizing how great a contribution they were making to the well-being of the community. The survey showed also what an immense task it would be to reorganize and coördinate these in order to make them as efficient as possible and at the same time assure their development along lines that would keep them abreast of every modern sociological development.

Only that the archbishop himself was so deeply intent on the matter and was resolved to make it the outstanding work of his archiepiscopacy the task ahead might have seemed almost deterring from its magnitude and the immense number of details associated with it. The archbishop was persuaded, however, that the Catholics of the archdiocese could be made to feel pardonable pride in the development of their charities and at the same time acquire a solidarity in diocesan work that would mean much both for themselves and for the poor. He proceeded to arouse the charitable feelings of his people and over three hundred parishes were appealed to, an active canvass of all their parishioners made and the Catholics of New York as a consequence came to have a consciousness of their power for good such as they had never had before. The pastoral letters of His Grace contained the strongest kind of urging of the duty of charity. Charity was not a luxury to be indulged for the sake of the good feeling that came with it, but an obligation that must not be neglected. Some of these pastoral letters with regard to charity have elicited marked attention from leading Catholics everywhere throughout the country and it has even been said that His Grace of New York was making important contributions to the Church's literature of charity.

On May 1, 1920, "The Catholic Charities of the Archdiocese of New York" was inaugurated. The first steps were taken slowly. The work was not really in action until September. His Grace became president of the Catholic Charities and his Secretary for Charities became Executive Director. Under the secretary there were set up six divisions:

Families, Children, Health, Protective Care, Social Action and Finance. Each of these divisions was under a director charged to "organize, improve and extend" the works of his division. His whole time and energy were directed along this one line. Weekly staff conferences were held at which common problems were discussed and general policies of operation recommended. The idea was to accomplish the work in the best possible way with progress as the watchword. No wonder that the State Board of Charities in its report to the Legislature of the State of New York for the year 1920 characterized the formation of the Catholic Charities of the Archdiocese of New York as "the most significant and important event of the year in the field of charitable work."

Under the circumstances it is not surprising that the State Board of Charities coöperates very closely with the Catholic Charities. The organization of Catholic Charities permits of coöperation with other bodies and facilitates the securing of accurate and up-to-date information concerning all charitable activities of a national, state or municipal character by sending representatives to the various important conferences held on these subjects. During the very first year Catholic Charities was represented at the following conferences: National Conference of Social Work; National Conference of Catholic Charities; American Hospital Association (Annual Meeting); National Catholic Hospital Association; New York State Conference of Charities and Corrections; New Jersey State Conference of Charities and Corrections; National Conference of the Catholic Young Men's Diocesan Union; the Catholic Federation of Newman Clubs; City Conference of Charities and Corrections; City Conference on Unemployment; Monthly Committee Meetings for Dispensary Development; Monthly Conference on Immigration; Private Conference of Catholic, Jewish and Protestant Rooming Agencies; Private Conference on Homeless Men and Youths; Private Conference on Financial Federation; Catholic Charities Conference in Toronto; National Meeting—National Council of Catholic Women. Nothing shows better than a list like this how hard a task it is to keep in touch with modern social service activities.

Realizing the great number of Catholics engaged in social work for private or public agencies and at the same time the splendid opportunity afforded by organizing this group with so many common interests, Catholic Charities instituted the Mulry Club as a social and vocational clearing house. Within a year some six hundred members were enrolled and much good has been accomplished. The name of the late Thomas Mulry who accomplished so much for Catholic charity in New York and whose example well deserved to be perpetuated was thus brought before social workers of this generation.

The six major Divisions of Catholic Charities proceeded with their task finding ever new work to do. The Division of Families concerned with the relief of the poor in their homes was organized in connection with the Conferences of St. Vincent de Paul which for years have been the Catholic relief agencies of the diocese. Four district offices were established to coördinate the relief work and avoid duplication of effort. County agents were appointed outside the city to direct relief work and make the various resources of public and private charitable agencies available to Catholics. Parish censuses were made and the status of all the Catholics especially in the poorer quarters of the city came to be well known.

The Division of Children having under its direction thirty-two Child Caring Homes has drawn up a set of standards that are being generally adopted by all these Homes. These standards are placing them in the first rank. The result has been a close and cordial coöperation. During the first year the orphan asylum buildings at Kingsbridge was sold to the

United States government to be used as a hospital for wounded and ailing soldiers thus helping the authorities to meet an urgent need. The children had to be transferred but these transfers were made in half the time allotted by the government and enlisted the highest commendation from the government officials and the board of trustees of the orphan asylum. The most important element for reorganization has been the installation in the large congregate Homes of the small group system for child care which practically makes them equivalent to the Homes on the Cottage Plan. This plan is regarded as the ideal by state officials and experts in social work in general. A special inspector of the children's homes and a dietitian from the office of Catholic Charities have done much to standardize and improve their service. All this has been done as well as the remodeling of buildings in conference with representatives from the State Board of Charity.

The day nurseries for the care of children during the day when their mothers have to be at work have been very largely developed. Altogether there are some twenty-seven of these and they are no longer merely day boarding houses for children but they are rendering a well defined service of health and education. A dietitian regulates the diet and teaches the youngsters and through them their mothers sound principles of nutrition and good habits of health and sanitation. There are kindergartners from the Board of Education and recreation teachers from Catholic Charities. It is in these day nurseries particularly that the Catholic Charities of the archdiocese accomplish their most significant work.

The Division of Health has supervision over twenty-two hospitals, four convalescent homes, and three orders of nursing Sisters which constitute the health unit of the archdiocese. A Central Bureau of Information and Service helps parochial clergy to place the sick with whom they come in contact and two new convalescent homes have been opened, one for men and one for women. Chaplain service has been improved in the non-Catholic hospitals by the recruiting of a band of fifty priests who volunteer to visit the sick in their free time. Close contact and cordial coöperation have been maintained with the State Board of Charities and Department of Public Welfare.

The organization of this Division is particularly wise and prudent. The central organization never assumes financial responsibility for the care of any patient in one of the Catholic hospitals although it refers many cases for treatment. Every Catholic hospital must make some provision for the care of

the poor or it has no special reason for existence.
Unless it is charitable it is not Catholic. The financial assistance given to hospitals is granted when it
is needed in order to maintain high standards of
efficiency and not in consideration of the number of
charitable cases it receives. Hundreds of thousands
of dollars have been appropriated for hospitals for
necessary improvements and extension to their service during the past six years. The hospitals in turn
have assumed their share of responsibility toward
the problem of poverty and have gladly accepted for
free care the poor whose cases have been found deserving. In fact their charitable contributions have
been far in excess of any assistance they have received. The people of the diocese have contributed
to the general charities fund out of which hospitals
have been helped when necessary and they in turn
have given to the people a generous and efficient
service. The quality of that service is best tested
by the approval they have received from the City
and State Departments of Health and Charities,
from the American College of Surgeons and the diocesan supervising body. During the past year over
33,000 patients have been treated in the hospitals.
Only about one in three paid in full for the service
received. The Department of Public Welfare of
the city paid in part for one in ten of these patients.

Some 9,000 made some part payment in proportion to their means. Nearly 8,000 made no payment whatever. Many of these free patients were of the type that remained for a long period in the hospitals so that altogether nearly 335,000 days of service were given to the poor free of charge. This service is made possible because Catholic hospital maintenance charges are not so high as others since the Sisters receive no salaries and manage most economically, and secondly because well-to-do people who know the situation and realize the demands that are made upon the hospital Sisters make donations for their work. Indeed many who thus donate every year are in but very moderate circumstances but they have a true sense of charity. The out-patient departments of the hospitals care for still more. Last year some 17,000 patients were cared for. These dispensaries prevent great economic waste and restore numbers to physical fitness who might otherwise become hospital patients. This work is improving and extending all the time and is accomplishing more and more good.

All this the Cardinal Archbishop's reorganization of charity has rendered easy of accomplishment and made ever so much more efficient. There is a sense of family coöperation in all the work that bears the stamp of true charity. There are many

other agencies which under the cardinal's encouragement are accomplishing great benefit. He is
very much interested in the communities of nursing
Sisters who visit the sick poor in their homes. Last
year these nurses cared for nearly 3,000 patients
spending on them over $10,000 in relief, but caring
for them and their sick rooms and making the lot
of the sick ever so much more bearable. This
service relieves the strain not only on the general
hospitals but also on the hospitals for incurables.
Were it not for the work of these Visiting Nurses
many incurable patients would be obliged to enter
the City Home. On acute cases the Sisters remain all day and even nurse through the night,
while they are able to visit a number of chronic
cases in a day. Lay Auxiliaries raise the necessary
funds. Appropriations are made from the general
charity fund when needed but the lay auxiliary work
is encouraged and last year the Auxiliary of the
Dominican Sisters * of the Sick Poor furnished suf-

---

* Without the Sisterhoods the accomplishment of all this social
work by Catholic Charities would be quite impossible. Besides
they afford the opportunity for children to be educated and re-
ligiously trained. The value of this for the state is coming to
be more and more recognized in the midst of the crime wave of
our day. Religion is the great stabilizing element for social
order. In this country there are probably about 75,000 sisters
who are devoted to the work of charity and of education. If
they were to receive on the average $1,000 a year each, which,
almost needless to say, would represent a very meager and
miserly payment for their services, they would receive some

ficient funds for the work of the Sisters though the preceding year an appropriation of $5,000 was needed.

The cardinal encouraged the foundation of a new religious congregation under the name of Parish Visitors whose principal duty is visiting the poor in their homes. The members of the congregation do not wear a conventional religious garb but are dressed quietly in dark clothes and make their visits to the homes not only during the day time but also in the evening. They are thus enabled to meet all the members of the family including those who may be at work during the day and are of help to them in the solution of their problems. All the members of the Parish Visitors are trained social workers and are required to take lectures in social service in Fordham University School of Social Service. They help the parish priest to know his people better, they complete the census of Catholics in each

---

$75,000,000 a year. What they get is just sufficient for board and clothes and proper support, so that the congregation can receive young members and train them and take care of the older ones who are superannuated. This large sum is the contribution which the Sisters make to education and charity in this country annually. The principal that at 5 per cent interest would provide an annual income of $75,000,000 is $1,500,000,000. Almost needless to say, this is several times the endowment of all our great institutions of education and charity in this country. By giving themselves to the work, the religious have endowed Catholic charities and education much more than millionaires have done for secular institutions.

parish, and they accomplish very much for the solution of social difficulties. They have practically
re-created in the modern time the order of dea-
conesses of the early Church and have provided a
vocation for many young women who feel the call
to the spiritual life and yet have profound sympathy for their fellow mortals and want to be of as
much assistance to them as possible. They com-
bine the spirit of Martha and Mary, of prayer and
of service, in a remarkable way, and their success
has been very gratifying to the cardinal's heart.

Almost needless to say the example of such self-
sacrificing work for others exerts a great influence
over those who come in contact with it. Example
means ever so much more than precept and the
cordial simple way in which these women go about
doing good lifts up the hearts of the poor and
touches deeply the hearts of those in better circumstances who are brought in touch with their work.
The social consolation which the visits of such
women afford lessens social unrest and minimizes
the tendency to social disorder. There are two
other sisterhoods whose principal work it is to visit
the sick poor and they feel that they are the object
of the most tender regard of His Eminence and
that their work is considered to be of very special
significance in the great labor of charity which he

thinks the most important duty of the cardinal arch-bishop.

The Division of Protective Care is accomplish-ing such good work in New York City where the problems it faces are so complicated, that it has at-tracted the attention of social workers everywhere. What has been done by the Catholic Charities Pro-bation Bureau of the Court of General Sessions has been publicly commended by the judges. Their ap-proval is in the official records of the court. Scien-tific analysis and treatment underlie all the case work of the Bureau. Individual treatment is given the problems of each man and a plan is made aim-ing at his complete rehabilitation. The reorganiza-tion of the Catholic Charities Probation Bureau, inspired as it was by religious and patriotic motives and urged by the cardinal himself because he is deeply interested in every phase of helpfulness for his people, has resulted in a work of genuine com-munity service.

In the reorganization of parole work for men, modern scientific methods of proved value are utilized and the workers have all received a thor-ough technical training. A report is given to the Board of Pardons as to the home conditions, the employment he will be able to secure and the history of his career of every prisoner whose case comes before the Board. New features have thus been initiated in parole work by the Catholic Protective Society. Over one thousand men are under supervision, five hundred of whom were discharged as having satisfactorily completed their terms and conditions of parole while about a hundred were declared delinquent. Employment was found for over three hundred.

The work with the women criminals has been equally or perhaps even more successful. Nearly 90 per cent of the women under direction made good with over a thousand cases handled during the year. This may be considered an absolute demonstration of the success of parole and probation work properly conducted. The report of the Catholic Charities for the year 1925 suggests that "it would be interesting to compare these figures with the percentage of success obtained by an equal number of the graduates of any six representative institutions for higher education." Close contact between supervisors and supervised is the largest factor in producing these gratifying results. In the parole cases this contact is begun long before the girl leaves the institution, so that by the time she is ready to be released the worker is fully acquainted with her and can plan intelligently for her future. The spiritual factors for reform are particularly insisted on and the cardinal has always emphasized the necessity for recourse to character rebuilding by faithful attendance at religious duties.

The Division of Social Action has charge of social activities of various kinds. There are boys' and girls' clubs and summer camps and Newman Clubs and Junior Newman Clubs for students at the universities and high schools, there is an employment department and a room registry as well as girls' residences and immigrant homes, and then there are the boy scouts and settlement houses and welfare centers and guilds. As an example of the extent of this development it may be noted that for the Portuguese residents of New York there are two clubs established by the St. Anthony's Welfare Guild, one for boys at St. Raphael's and one for girls in the lower Bronx. Both clubs have orchestras and a complete course in all branches of music for those who desire them.

The County Committees have accomplished good work in the counties outside New York City and their most important function is "impenetration," that is, the leavening of the whole population by a comparatively small but representative group thoroughly imbued with the true philosophy of Catholic Charities. The work of these County Committees also includes Newman Clubs at Vassar and Eastman Colleges in Poughkeepsie and at the Kingston High School. The subcommittees on health continue their excellent and self-sacrificing labor for the school children of their respective communities and the subcommittees on rural activities keep the general committee well informed as regards country conditions.

The Division of Finance secures the sinews of war for the whole campaign of charity. The cardinal's committee comprising over fifteen thousand laymen and women in three hundred and sixteen parishes collected nearly a million of dollars in the Charity drive of the very first year. Altogether during the past six years some five millions of dollars have been gathered. Donations have come to Catholic Charities in larger sums from other sources which have provided an additional nearly $100,000 a year. The Altman Foundation through Colonel Friedsam gave $15,000 last year; the Elks $1,000; the Friendly Sons of St. Patrick, $500; the Fourth Degree Knights of Columbus, $1,000; the archdiocesan Holy Name Societies, $500; the Holy Name Society of the New York Police Department, $150. Even more surprising as indicating the thoroughgoing feeling of appreciation for the cardinal's reorganization of the Catholic Charities of New York is the fact that the charity committee of the

Masonic Order of Manhattan and Richmond donated $2,000. Five hundred dollars more came from the Robert Boyd Ward Fund, Inc. The New York *Times* Christmas Appeal for "The One Hundred Neediest Cases" and the New York *Evening Post* "Christmas Appeal for Aged Couples" contributed to Catholic Charities nearly $40,000 feeling that through this agency it would be spent to the best advantage.

The report of the Division of Finance shows that very little of the money obtained for charity is spent on administration and that altogether scarcely more than one out of every ten cents is used up in the expense of distribution. Of each dollar contributed three cents is spent for printing and other material used in making the appeal, three cents in parish organization, one cent in acquiring information as to conditions and the needs of those who are to be benefited, four cents in administration, two cents in county agents. As the result of this genuine economy eighty-seven cents of every dollar given to charity finds its way directly into the hands of those who need it.

All this has been accomplished because the cardinal archbishop of New York wanted to make this service to the community the most important feature of his administration of the great archdiocese of

New York. He eminently deserves the title that has been applied to him of "the cardinal of charity." All this has come out of the warmth of his own heart-felt sympathy for. the poor and the needy and his cordial recognition of the fact that charity is the greatest work that man can do. As he himself says, quoting St. Augustine, "Charity is the way of God to men and the way of men to God."

The cardinal has emphasized above all the common bond of sympathy that exists in the spirit of helpfulness, fellowship and charity. "The rich and the poor, the strong and the weak, the great and the humble, the free man and those in chains have all a common contact in the charity of Christ." This he said in his Pastoral of Easter, 1925. And then lest it should be thought that the charity which he tries to foster so sedulously represents in any sense of the word an effort to conjure social evils by the panacea of condescending aid, he repudiated any such outlook upon charity. He said, "There is a pronounced tendency, at the present hour, to test nearly every human relation, from the cradle to the grave, by a purely economic valuation. It is, of course, the result of materialism, pure and simple. No more reactionary step, in the light of history, could be imagined. In the field of charity, were the economic standard to prevail over the spiritual standard, which has stood the shock of centuries of assault and conflict, then no longer would it be nobler and more blessed to give than to receive. Rather the philosophy of might against right, of selfishness against kindliness, of indulgence against duty, and of sin against virtue would be sanctioned and followed."

Undoubtedly the place of Cardinal Hayes in the history of his time in the archdiocese of New York will be desumed from his deep interest in charity. Personally this constitutes the best summary of his character. Those who know him best think of him as the personification of charity. This is not at all of the nature of condescension but is a genuine sentiment of the dearness of all men to him because of the Fatherhood of God and the brotherhood of man. Undoubtedly if he is spared to reach the years of his predecessor he will change the social aspect of New York in many ways and will add greatly to the happiness and well-being of the community. Christ Himself said that the supreme sign of His Church was that "The Gospel is preached to the poor." This He told to the disciples of John the Baptist when they came to inquire what they should tell their master about Him. Cardinal Hayes has the feeling that the poor we shall always have about us, but if they are saved from the evils of poverty, they may, contented in it find happiness even beyond what is granted to those who possess the world's goods. And he has made it his special mission in life to bring this about as far as it may be done in the great archdiocese of New York.

INDEX

Ablutions, 7
Adirondacks, 35
Æschylus, 35
Aglipayan schism, 230, 233
Albany, 34, 35, 36; bishop
  of, 130
Altman Foundation, 338
Alverno High School, 273
American, characteristically,
  88; right-minded, 82;
  true, 83
American College of Sur-
  geons, 329
American Consistory, 284
American Hospital Associa-
  tion, 326
*American, The Making of
  an,* 95
Americanism, 53, 269; hy-
  phenated, 106
Americans, Portuguese, 18
Ancient Academy of Arcadia,
  257
"Apostle of the Point," 63
Archipelago, 236
Area, 267
Army, Catholics in, 306;
  English, 8
Arthur, President, 50
Ashland, 222
Associated Catholic Chari-
  ties of Chicago, 263
Assumption Academy, 239
Athens, 3
Augustinians, 212
Austria, 18

Authority without despotism,
  116
Axiére, Bishop of, 33

Bailey, Archbishop, 78
Baltimore, 5, 37, 68, 86;
  coadjutor of, 78; Third
  Plenary Council of, 81, 89
Bardstown, 5
Basil, 42
Belgæ, 229
Belgian missionaries, 228
Belgium, 54
Belloc, Hilaire, xv
Benedict XV, Pope, 241, 313
Benedictines, 254, 255
Biretta, 288
Bishop ordinary of Armed
  Forces of the United
  States, 307
"Bishops, nursery of," 120
"Bishop, the boy," 68
Board of Regents, 305
Bonanzo, Most Reverend
  John, 313
Boston, archdiocese review,
  195; coadjutor archbishop
  of, 192; College, 177
Bottomley, Dr. John, 200
Boursand, Father, 177
Bowen, Reverend John M.,
  258, 259
Brady, Thomas, James T.,
  John R., 4; School, 4
Breckenridge, 37

(1)

OF THE SPIRIT

PEARL: A STUDY IN SPIRITUAL DRYNESS.
By Sister M. Madeleva.

After a careful study of the considerations of other scholars, Sister M. Madeleva gives her own interpretation of this beautiful and famous old English poem which she sees as an allegory of a man's struggle for faith against doubt and evil.

CHAUCER'S NUNS.
By Sister M. Madeleva.

In this volume Sister M. Madeleva reveals besides fine scholarship and, as a Catholic nun, her unique point of view, a vivacity and charm of writing that is delightful.

KNIGHTS ERRANT
By Sister M. Madeleva.

A volume of lovely verses of nature and of spiritual experience. Bits of the world's life stand out, seen from the nun's viewpoint.

STARSHINE AND CANDLELIGHT.
By Sister Mary Angelita.

Reflected in the poems is a spirit of delicacy and culture fired to poetic expression by a keen sense of beauty. Some are purely personal lyrics, the record of a mood or emotion. Others are translations of Hugo, Bourget, and other famous poets.

TROUBADOURS OF PARADISE.
By Sister M. Eleanore.

Presents the saints from a new point of view—human beings who have had to face in their lives the same problems that meet us all. It is not only through their martyrdom that these men and women inspire us, but through the conduct of their lives day by day.

D. APPLETON AND COMPANY

New York   London